27.4.84

ENERGY, ENVIRONMENT AND DEVELOPMENT IN AFRICA 1

ENERGY AND DEVELOPMENT IN KENYA:
OPPORTUNITIES AND CONSTRAINTS

Edited by
PHIL O'KEEFE, PAUL RASKIN AND STEVE BERNOW

Published by
THE BEIJER INSTITUTE
The Royal Swedish
Academy of Sciences
Stockholm, Sweden

THE SCANDINAVIAN INSTITUTE
OF AFRICAN STUDIES
Uppsala, Sweden

The series "Energy, Environment and Development in Africa" is published jointly by the Beijer Institute and the Scandinavian Institute of African Studies with financial support from the Swedish
International Development Authority (SIDA). This book together
with a series of companion volumes reports on a Beijer Institute
study, the "Kenyan Fuelwood Project", undertaken jointly with the
Government of Kenya.

ISSN 0281-8515
ISBN 91-7106-225-4

© the Beijer Institute and the Scandinavian Institute of
African Studies 1984

Printed in Sweden by
Bohusläningens AB, Uddevalla 1984

FOREWORD

The material presented in this Volume is a summary of the findings of the Kenyan Fuelwood Project. The detailed analytical data on which these findings rest are contained in a series of technical volumes to be published later.

It is worth recording how the Project came into being because its long period of incubation prior to start-up marks the gradual shifting of public perceptions about energy and energy planning. As late as 1978 the belief was still widely held that of all the primary energy consumed in Kenya, about 80 per cent came from imported oil. But by 1980, the role of wood, charcoal and crop-wastes as fuels became generally recognized. By this time, it was being suggested that maybe as much as three-quarters of Kenya's annual primary energy was consumed as wood, charcoal and crop-residues with only about 20 per cent coming from oil. In other words, the predominant use of biomass-fuels by ordinary households for cooking, space-heating and even lighting also began to be accepted as "energy". This put the 25 per cent or so used in the commercial and industrial sectors into a more balanced perspective.

In November 1977, the recently founded Beijer Institute began work on Energy and Development issues as part of the research remit mapped out for it by its International Advisory Board. Since the energy problems in East Africa seemed at that time to be critical, it was decided to embark on a long-term study of energy/development issues in East Africa using Kenya as a case-study. Discussions began with Kenyan scientists in Stockholm and Nairobi in February 1978. Future energy provision was already under active consideration within Kenya and discussions led to an agreement with the Kenyan Energy Sub-committee to develop a two-phase seminar. Under Phase I, the National Council for Science and Technology (NCST) of Kenya planned a Kenyan National Energy Symposium to identify the main energy "actors" within Kenya and to initiate a forum for energy debate. This was held very successfully in November 1978.

Under Phase II, the Beijer Institute would plan an International Workshop of a technical nature to provide a fact-base for elucidating the energy-policy issues of Kenya. This was held in Nairobi in May 1979 with wide local and international attendance. The Workshop was organized by the Beijer Institute and co-sponsored by the Kenyan Academy of Sciences and the United Nations Environment Programme who subsequently published the Proceedings.

As a result of this, the Government suggested that the Beijer Institute explore further the major theme of its Workshop - the role of fuelwood as a focal point in the energy economy of Kenya - and the preliminary discussions with the Ministry of Power and Communications were eventually transferred to the Ministry of Energy, newly formed after the October 1979 election. The Ministry required a detailed work-plan to be prepared and submitted to it for discussion prior to our embarking upon the work itself which should be a pre-investment study for a large rolling programme of future energy provision, concentrating on the place of biomass in the total energy-matrix of Kenya.

Accordingly, with the help of some "seed-money" from the Swedish Agency for Research Co-Operation with Developing Countries (SAREC), an International Reference Group of energy specialists selected by the Beijer Institute met in Stockholm in January 1980 to discuss the possibilities of mounting such a wide-ranging systems study of Kenya's future energy requirements. A further Group Meeting in March evaluated and adopted a document to be forwarded to the Kenyan Government who approved it. By August 1980 initial funding had been secured by the generosity of the Royal Netherlands Ministry of Foreign Affairs and the German Appropriate Technology Exchange of the German Agency for Technical Co-operation (GTZ). The project was launched in December, 1980. Both the Swedish International Development Authority (SIDA) and the United States Agency for International Development (USAID) subsequently contributed resources to complete the funding needed for the Project.

It took almost 3 years of careful preparatory work to develop sensible analytical goals, to write detailed research programmes and to build constituencies providing official moral and financial support for action both in Kenya and among donor countries. At the time it seemed a painfully slow and frustrating process. But reflecting now upon those years, I think we all expected that the changes in public perception, which were needed to legitimize our approach and allow the Project to be born, would happen much too quickly.

The work was comprehensive. Data on commercial supply was carefully calculated with officials from the Ministry of Energy and the Central Bureau of Statistics. Commercial demand data was more difficult to obtain but East African Power and Light (EAPL) and the oil companies gave valuable help and allowed access to sales figures. Important demand information was also provided by parastatal corporations and the larger private consumers. It was, however, the problem of obtaining good data on supply and demand in the non-commercial energy sector that concerned the research team.

From the beginning of the analysis, the research team were preoccupied with issues of non-commercial energy. Although there were preliminary and conflicting estimates of fuelwood's contribution to the total energy balance of Kenya, it was clear that it was the significant resource. The national demand surveys for rural and urban households and informal industry, largely conducted with the Central Bureau of Statistics, were a major effort. They allowed an accurate picture to be drawn of end-use consumption patterns across different social classes. This process of data collection and analysis was supported by twelve detailed village-level case studies which provided an understanding of fuel procurement and consumption within the household economy for every ecological zone.

Much detailed work was undertaken to analyse all aspects of non-commercial supply. The Kenya Rangeland Ecological Monitoring Unit (KREMU) and the Department of Forestry of the University of Nairobi provided strong support in remote sensing, photo interpretation and mensuration exercises. Within the Project, the analysis of non-commercial supply, like the analysis of non-commercial demand, was a departure from the usual perfunctory treatment of traditional fuels: it allowed a comprehensive analysis of the dominant energy sector in Kenya. It also allowed analysis to be performed on associated problems such as soil erosion.

All this work produced a snapshot of Kenya's energy balance for 1980. The problem, however, was to convert this static picture into one moving forward with time. The Central Bureau of Statistics and the Ministry of Economic Development and Planning provided invaluable help in discussions of demography and growth targets respectively. The Ministry of Agriculture gave assistance in outlining the implications of the Government of Kenya's food policy. It was, however, the Ministry of Energy that encouraged the team to build the end-use energy accounting system into a policy tool for analysis and planning of programmatic options. This volume contains a synthesis of that analysis, a synthesis that has permitted the development of an energy policy in Kenya. But the impact of the work goes far beyond questions of wood and energy not least because it focuses development initiative back on the high potential land.

Work did not end with the production of the policy analysis. Detailed consideration was given to the costs and benefits of the programmatic options. A series of interventions was proposed, adopted and is currently being implemented. In particular, the work on agroforestry is a significant departure which holds great hope for the future. The importance of agroforestry to integrated energy planning in developing countries cannot be over-emphasised.

In retrospect, many of the broad conclusions, which are applicable to other African countries, seem commonplace. These conclusions, however, mark a significant shift from the accepted wisdom of energy planning and suggest:

(a) that if terms of trade between developed and developing countries continue to stagnate there will be little capital available to increase the proportion of commercial energy in the national energy budget. Consequently, biomass utilization will increase in absolute terms and, in some cases, relative terms;

(b) since fuelwood is the most important biomass energy source, increasing pressure will be placed on it by a rising population. Consequently, there will be increased cutting of standing stocks of wood because annual yields are insufficient to support demand;

(c) that, given the accelerated urban demand for charcoal as a result of rapid urbanization, accelerating wood removal will occur as charcoal making often causes the complete destruction. of whole trees. Consequently, attention should be given to the provision of fuelwood belts around urban areas;

(d) if, as we believe, rural biomass consumption is largely based on trees outside the forest and rarely involves the destruction of whole trees, the more densely populated high-potential regions will experience greatest pressures. Consequently, it will be necessary to evolve programmes that provide biomass energy from <u>within</u> farms;

(e) that there appear to be many problems associated with the countrywide diffusion of new stoves, and so there are structural constraints that inhibit fuelwood conservation. Consequently, it will be necessary to concentrate stove diffusion efforts on the proven market of urban stoves;

(f) that, given the lack of capital for technology and the problems of technology transfer, conservation efforts in the commercial fuel sector will have a slow impact. Consequently, careful analysis of future fuel-technology combinations is necessary if national enterprises wish to remain viable.

These points can be summarized as follows. Over the next twenty years, commercial fuel consumption will not substantially change its percentage share of the national energy budget. Furthermore, the capital limits on conservation programmes will continue to force much of the cash burden onto the recurrent budget. Fuelwood consumption will grow consuming increasing amounts of wood stocks. But it is the drive to urbanization, and the consequent demand for charcoal, that will cause acute problems of wood-destruction in an energy economy that remains dominated by the hewers of wood.

The task has been long and difficult to carry out but has I think yielded many valuable fruits for future energy policy. As its initiator, I am particularly pleased that a follow-up programme under the auspices of the Netherlands Foreign Ministry - the Kenyan Woodfuel Development Programme - will use the findings of the Project to learn how to set up a self-sustaining "grass-roots" tree planting process for woodfuels among peasant farmers. This has been started by the Beijer Institute in the Kakamega District of Kenya.

Apart from this, reflecting on the Project's germination, growth and its fruits, what remains for me is a sense of great gratitude, and pride in the tremendous exhilaration and commitment obviously felt by all those who shared in the work of the Project and carried it out so splendidly.

Gordon T. Goodman, Director.

ACKNOWLEDGMENTS

The Beijer Institute could not have carried out this Project without the assistance of many helpful people and organizations. Apart from the various agencies already mentioned in the Foreword, I would like to thank many individuals for their support, in particular David N. Mwiraria and Francis M. Ligale, Permanent Secretaries in the Ministry of Energy. William M. Mbote, as the first Deputy Secretary in the Ministry of Energy, gave initial advice and support to the Project and this was continued by Francis Mayeka. Two stalwarts of the Project were, Patrick N. Nyoike and Lincoln Bailey, who respectively operated as co-manager and secretary to the research, and who rightly deserve credit for interpreting the results into policy.

I am indebted to the sponsors of the Project. William Floor, Arjan Hamburger, Rob de Voss and Johan Boer of the Royal Netherlands Foreign Ministry deserve special credit for their intellectual, financial and moral support. Hans-Wilhelm von Haugwitz of the German Appropriate Technology Exchange (of GTZ) provided similar support. Alison Herrick, John Blumgard, Satish Shah and Joe Pastic of the United States Agency for International Development (USAID) and Lars-Olof Edström and Karen Wohlin of the Swedish International Development Agency provided additional funds and new lines of inquiry. To them, their colleagues and the Dutch, German, American and Swedish governments, the Institute extends its gratitude. I warmly thank our Chairman, Professor Jack Hollander, and the Board of the Beijer Institute, for much advice and support.

In the preparation of the research programme helpful advice was received from Turi Hammer, Bill Morgan, Olle Edquist, Jöran Fries, Anders Rapp, Lil Lundgren, Bill Marin, Mikael Grut, Tony Pryor, Tom Tuschak, Ariane van Buren, Nicolai Herlofson, and Richard and Philip Leakey. Many other people gave of their time and effort and gratitude is extended to them.

Two organizations were central to the completion of this work namely the Graduate School of Geography, Clark University, and the Energy Systems Research Group (ESRG), Boston. At Clark, a large debt of gratitude is owed to Len Berry and Don Shakow and, among the many graduate students, to Ellen Hughes-Cromwick. The ESRG, as a group, provided much analytical support, particularly David White and Jim Goldstein who worked, under pressure, to review and carefully check all numerical data. And, of course, Paul Raskin and Steve Bernow "lived with" the Project for a period of three years.

I am deeply indebted to the central members of the field team, in particular to Richard Hosier, who built up the Project from on-the-ground experience. The team included Keith Openshaw, Dan Weiner, Tom Harris, Nancy Folbre, F. A. Kene, Lousie Buck, Diana Lee-Smith (Mazingira Institute), Berry van Gelder, Gunnar Poulsen, David Western, James Ssemakula, Tom Dunne, Brian Aubry, Mike Rainey, Tom Hart, Lee Schipper, Matt Milukas, Krishna

Prasad, Keith Brown, Calestous Juma, Nick Highton, Carolyn Barnes, Ben Wisner, Jim Ellis and the Turkana Research Unit, Jean Ensminger, Angela Haugerud, Jane Hayes, Judy Johnson, Faith Oleche, Diane Perlov, Bjorn Andersson, Jöran and Ingrid Fries, Cynthia Jensen, Cara Seiderman, Wim van Lierop, Lamen van Veldhuizen, Paul Kerkhof, Wim van der Donk and Kapiyo. John, James and Solomon, the masters of Kuni Kastle, kept the team in line and Sture Persson provided diplomatic avenues when all else was closed. And to those many, many Kenyans who served as interviewers and to those who provided much valuable information, we all owe a debt of gratitude not only for their unique contributions but for the tremendous optimism they inspired in us all.

Elaine Watts and June Summers provided cartographic and Word processing skills respectively. Their patience, efficiency and accuracy helped the rapid publication of this manuscript.

Finally, I want to thank Lars Kristoferson for his constant advice and support. But we both agree that our greatest debt of gratitude by far we owe to our colleague Phil O'Keefe, who managed the Project, from organizing the preparation of the initial research programme in 1980, through fieldwork and analysis, to the political discussions and the publication of the material. He was an inspiration to everyone connected with the work and I cannot imagine how the Project could have been carried through without him.

Gordon T.Goodman
Director.

ENERGY AND DEVELOPMENT IN KENYA:

OPPORTUNITIES AND CONSTRAINTS

CONTENTS

LIST OF TABLES

Page

LIST OF FIGURES

Page

CHAPTER 1. INTRODUCTION

        The purpose of this study is to contribute to the process of
timely energy planning in Kenya. The achievement of near and long
term development objectives requires that energy resources of the
proper type and magnitude be available to sustain the various
sectors of the Kenyan economy. Indeed, as population growth
combines with escalating world fossil fuel prices, depletion of
indigenous wood fuel resources, and increasing constraints on
high quality agricultural land availability, the need for
appropriate policy intervention becomes increasingly urgent.
Moreover, such planning must occur on a regional as well as
national basis, in order that development goals for balanced
growth be reached.
        This volume, complemented by a set of nine volumes of
supporting material, contains the summary findings of the Beijer
Fuelwood Cycle Study. As the project title suggests, the primary
focus is on clarifying the problems attendant upon the
accelerating depletion of Kenya's indigenous wood resource and
assessing a range of policy initiatives which could address that
problem.
        Problems of fuelwood supply and demand, however, are linked
closely to other factors such as demographic trends, alternative
fuel availability, social patterns, economic projections, biomass
availability, and government policies. In this investigation,
fuelwood issues are placed within an integrated and inclusive
energy planning framework. Consequently, the project has required
and generated a prodigious output of relevant information. Basic
data on the pattern of energy use in Kenya have been developed,
much of this gathered through field surveys. Long-range forecasts
of energy supply and demand at a high level of sectoral and
regional disaggregation have been prepared. For this purpose, an
original computer-based resource planning capability, offering a
unique emphasis on land-use and biomass availability, has been
created. By using these methods, trouble spots in adequate
supply/demand balancing over time have been quantitatively
identified. Candidate technologies, projects, and policies which
could begin to solve such problems, particularly with respect to
fuelwood, have been assessed. The time frame for which these
analyses were undertaken is the 1980-2000 period.
        The body of this volume is devoted to summarizing these
methods and results. Other volumes are listed in Table 1.1.

The Beijer Institute Fuelwood Cycle Project.

        Late in 1977, the International Board of the Institute for
Energy and Human Ecology (The Beijer Institute) of the Royal
Swedish Academy of Sciences adopted "Improved Energy Utilization

TABLE 1.1

Supporting Technical Volumes

1. Environmental Impacts of Wood Use in Kenya.

2. Forestry Issues in Kenyan Development.

3. Economic Appraisal of Fuelwood Policy.

4. Issues in the Diffusion of Appropriate Energy Technology.

5. Village Studies of Energy Utilization.

6. Rural Household Energy Consumption.

7. Urban Energy Consumption.

8. Issues in Kenyan Energy Planning.

9. Energy Accounting in Developing Countries.

(These volumes will be published later in the year in this same series).

in Developing Countries" as a priority area for research and development studies. In line with this priority and in light of long-established links between the Academy and Kenyan scientific institutes, it was decided to embark on a long-term study of energy and development issues in East Africa with Kenya serving as a case study. Discussions began with the Kenyan authorities in February 1978, leading to agreement with the Kenyan Energy Committee that a two-phase seminar be held. Under Phase 1, the Kenyan Academy of Sciences (KAS) planned a Kenyan National Energy symposium to identify the energy "actors" within Kenya and to initiate a forum for energy debate. This was held in November 1978. Under Phase 2, the Beijer Institute planned an International Workshop of a technical nature to provide a fact-base to elucidate energy policy issues in Kenya. This was held in Nairobi in May 1979. It was attended by Kenyan experts as well as participants from neighbouring countries and from overseas. The meeting was co-sponsored by the Kenyan Academy of Sciences and the United Nations Environment Program which later published the proceedings.

At this point, the Government of Kenya suggested that Beijer explore further the major theme of the workshop - the role of fuelwood as a focal point in the energy economy of Kenya. Liaison ultimately resided in the Ministry of Energy (created in 1980) which invited the Beijer Institute to:

(a) Prepare a detailed work plan for carrying out a systems study of the fuelwood cycle within the energy and development context of Kenya, using an International Reference Group for this work;

(b) Submit the plan for detailed discussion by the Ministry of Energy; then

(c) embark upon the systems study, which would be implemented as a pre-investment study for a large rolling programme of energy provision by a small team of international and Kenyan experts, coordinated by the Beijer Institute.

Accordingly, an International Reference Group of experts was selected by the Beijer Institute to meet in January and March 1980 in Stockholm. The final March meeting of the group approved a document which was cleared as a suitable statement and plan of the tasks needed to be implemented when carrying out the proposed systems study. This document formed the basis of a Work Plan for an Analysis of the Fuelwood Cycle in Kenya. The latter document was approved by the Government of Kenya in the summer of 1980. Funding for the project was provided by foreign assistance agencies representing the governments of the Netherlands, the Federal Republic of Germany, Sweden and the United States.

The project was intended to build on the existing knowledge base of the overall energy supply and demand situation in Kenya and, more particularly, the supply of and demand for fuelwood. Estimates undertaken prior to the Beijer Institute effort had indicated a fuelwood demand in Kenya ranging between a low value of 1 m³ per person and a high value of 2 m³ (1). A 1975 estimate of growth per annum at 2 per cent.(2) suggested that consumption exceeded annual production by the early 1970's. Further, the problem was perceived as embedded in a matrix of evolving demographic, economic, sociological, and ecological determinants.

The work plan, therefore, proposed the implementation of a systems study in three stages. The first stage would develop an energy account and projections for energy demand and supply. The second stage would identify the technical and socio-economic relationships affecting the demand and supply for fuelwood. The third phase would identify potential policy interventions which might be undertaken to enhance the net supply of fuelwood and to arrest depletion of stocks.

As mentioned earlier, the body of this book is devoted to summarizing the main issues and findings of the project effort. Specialized material on important aspects of the energy problem in Kenya, along with detailed documentation of data sources, field surveys, and computer analyses, are deferred to the series of technical books listed in Table 1.1.

Chapter 2 provides the broad backdrop of the inquiry. The relationship between economic development and energy consumption is considered in general terms, the performance and prospects for the Kenyan economy are discussed, and the broad issues required to inform long-range energy planning are identified. Chapter 3 summarizes the current energy flow in Kenya. Considerable quantitative detail is given on the structure of demand, with estimates of consumption disaggregated by user sector, fuel type, and selected end-use categories. Secondary conversion processes (primarily the production of charcoal, electricity, and petroleum) are characterized and the demands for primary sources of energy and imported energy forms reported.

Chapter 4 analyzes the basic features of fuelwood supply and demand in Kenya. The physical resource base is described in detail by considering the country as a composite of regions each of which in turn is broken down by ecological zone and then by land-use patterns. The threefold decomposition into regions, zones, and land-use categories permits detailed specification of wood stocks, yields, and availability. The current sufficiency of fuelwood supply and process of stock depletion is discussed. Moreover, this section also describes the other key aspect of land productivity, agricultural output. This is necessary, firstly to complete the picture of Kenya's overall performance and development objectives, and secondly, to identify potential areas of conflict between agricultural and wood production and their ecological consequences.

If chapters 3 and 4 give a snapshot of the current pattern
of consumption and supply of energy while chapter 5 presents a
motion picture of an evolution and transformation of this pattern
to the end of this century, given the contribution of present
trends. These projections of end-use demand, land-use patterns
and fuelwood resources serve as yardsticks for analyzing the
structure of future requirements in order to identify potential
resource inadequacies, and for testing the impacts of alternative
patterns and technologies which a preemptive energy policy might
induce. Chapter 5 is therefore labelled the "Present Trends" or
"Base Case", since the projections in it assume no major
deviation from existing energy policy. The Base Case, by
indicating what is forthcoming in the absence of major new energy
policy initiatives, shows that major inconsistencies will soon
occur, requiring significant policy initiatives, and provides a
reference point to aid in developing programme targets for such
initiatives.

Chapter 6 reviews the major strategies for improving the
long-term energy picture in Kenya. The basic characteristics of
each option are identified and their merits in the Kenyan context
evaluated. In chapter 7, specific timetables and penetration
targets for implementing the most promising of these strategies
are developed. These are presented as "Policy Case" projections
of supply and demand. These projections measure the impacts of
policy-induced transitions from present (Base Case) patterns. In
this manner, light is shed on the magnitude and repercussions of
any given strategy. The scale, range, and timing required of an
integrated energy programme begin to emerge and are summarized in
chapter 8.

CHAPTER 2. ENERGY IN THE KENYAN ECONOMY.

The following chapter aims to place the current technical investigation within the perspective of a broader planning context. First, general considerations on the relationship of energy to development are presented and a methodological moral drawn. Then, the nature and past performance of the Kenyan economy are summarized and future trends and goals discussed. Finally, basic issues in energy planning are outlined.

Energy and Development

Economic development has been linked historically to increasing energy consumption per capita. The progressive substitution of inanimate energy forms for human and animal power in agriculture, industry, and the household has characterized economies in growth. Additionally, inspection of energy to output relationships across nations, at a given point in time, reveals this phenomenon in its aggregate aspect.

The basic correlation between economic output and energy consumption is illustrated in Figure 2.1, where per capita energy consumption is plotted against per capita gross national product for each country (3). Only commercial energy forms (coal, petroleum, natural gas, hydroelectric, nuclear) are included in the energy/output plot of Figure 2.1, since reliable information on the so-called non-commercial sources (primarily wood based fuels, animal dung, and agricultural residues) is not available. While the developing countries have more than two-thirds of the world's population, they consume less than 20 per cent of total commercial energy. As we shall see, in Kenya today commercial energy comprises less than one-third of total energy supplies. Nevertheless, the figure indicates the relationship between increasing energy use and economic development.

Having noted this, however, the scatter in Figure 2.1 suggests that important caveats are in order. Among the less developed countries LDC's, there are wide variations in the pattern of development which lead to substantial spread in the relationship of energy to output. The OPEC countries of course have a special status. But even within the non-OPEC LDC's, such factors as the level and type of industrialization, the availability of indigenous energy sources, and the role of primary and agricultural exports play an important role in determining the precise energy requirements for growth. Furthermore, even within the industrialized countries, the earlier concept of a lock-step relationship between energy inputs and economic output clearly does not survive closer examination and has been abandoned by most analysts. The type and magnitude of energy required to produce a given set of goods can vary

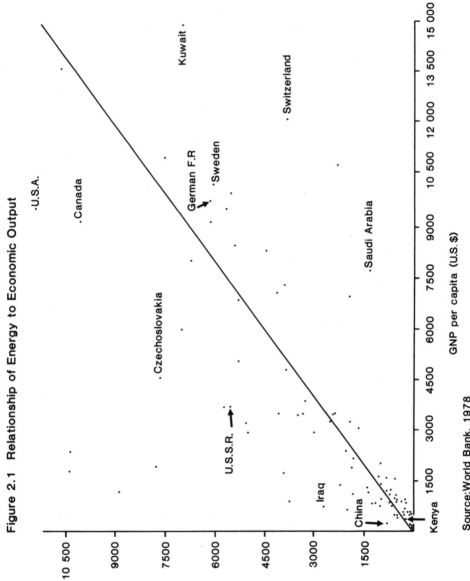

Figure 2.1 Relationship of Energy to Economic Output

Source:World Bank, 1978

widely depending on the process employed, the spatial configuration of supply and demand, and the efficiency of energy conversion. Indeed, least-cost strategies for achieving a given output show that energy consumption can be reduced dramatically and cost-effectively (4).

The less developed countries have an opportunity to incorporate levels of energy-use efficiency in their vehicles, buildings, and equipment at an early stage of development. The change in energy inputs associated with or required to effect a change in GNP need not follow the path marked by the solid line in Figure 2.1. Rather large growth in national economies can be accompanied by small increases in commercial energy requirements and vice-versa. Energy policy, to a considerable degree, can serve to manage the relationship of energy to growth. This is a theme to which we shall return below.

It is clear that the proper assessment of the energy requirements for economic growth must consider the detailed pattern of development in a given country. A larger set of basic development questions are raised by the energy issue. Does the 'modernization' of the rural sector necessitate a transition to commercial energy use? Should priority be given to commercial energy use in the industrial sector with the promise of faster GDP growth? How can limited high-quality land be used to supply both sufficient food and biomass? What is the most effective set of energy-related regulatory, pricing, and incentive policies to sustain development goals?

Two independent phenomena have in recent years underscored the urgency of resolving these dilemmas. These are the rapid increases in the price of petroleum and petrol products since 1973, and the depletion of fuelwood resources in rural areas with associated damage to the physical environment. Increased oil prices - as well as those of imported food, raw material and manufactured goods - have undermined the balance of payment accounts of oil-importing LDC's. Trade deficits have forced increases in debt levels, debt-servicing burdens, and taxes. Meanwhile, the need to expand economic activity becomes more urgent as population growth and rural-urban migration proceeds apace.

The barriers to increased energy independence are substantial. Research and development into alternative energy sources and technologies are costly, and generally are financed by scarce foreign capital. Even where available, the development of non-renewables such as tar sands, oil shales, and so on, requires massive allocation of scarce capital. Possible substitutes for high price oil (e.g., coal and natural gas) may experience comparable price increases.

The second problem mentioned - the "other energy crisis" - is the depletion of fuelwood in the rural areas. This issue shall be a primary focus of our analysis specific to Kenya. In general, the increasing inaccessibility of fuelwood puts severe stress on the rural economy as collection times and effort rise, fuel costs increase (e.g, as a result of charcoal substitution), and agricultural productivity is threatened. The latter impact can result when, in the absence of adequate development planning, the interrelated processes of deforestation, erosion, and loss of water-retention damage the structure and nutritional content of the soil. In addition, fuelwood scarcity may force households to use animal dung or crop residues for direct energy purposes rather than as agricultural inputs. Such practices alter the relationship between traditional energy inputs and agricultural resources with long-term repercussions.

The issue of agriculture and energy is of fundamental importance since the adoption of specific strategies here has important implications for the character of national development in general. Increasing agricultural output is an objective in all developing countries. Beyond the desire to improve the nutrition of the population, agricultural surpluses provide a basis for a growing urban economy and for export. Development of the rural sector is a key component in deepening and expanding demand and generating the savings from which development in general can occur.

The approach to agricultural development will depend on the level of modernization, resource endowment, development philosophy, and socio-cultural patterns in the countryside. Some countries emphasize large-scale mechanized agriculture, others emphasize small-scale labour-intensive farming, and some attempt the joint development of both strategies simultaneously. The large-scale approach requires, in addition to heavy capital outlays, high non-renewable energy inputs, including inorganic fertilizer.

By contrast, small-scale agriculture primarily uses fuelwood, small-scale water power, and human and animal power. Here, such techniques as the introduction of high yielding crop varieties, multiple cropping, more efficient irrigation, and intensive use of fertilizers are relied on to increase yields. More sophisticated use of rural biomass to provide the energy basis for raising agricultural productivity (e.g., producer gas driven pumps and motors) is a subject of emerging importance for development planning. Given the problem of fuelwood depletion, integrated strategies for enhancing both the biomass resource base and agricultural production are indicated. Otherwise, increasing demands for imported energy to fuel a rapidly increasing agricultural sector may interfere with development goals in other sectors which also rely on the importation of fuel, materials, and machinery from abroad. Limitations on foreign-exchange earnings, exacerbated by sky-rocketing fuel costs, place constraints on joint agricultural and industrial planning and growth targets.

Development theory has to date not explicitly incorporated the problem of the energy constraints to growth or the need to blend a realistic energy plan into the wider social and economic planning process. An adequate theory would have the ability to address such issues as the relationship between energy consumption and economic growth, the impact of the cost increase for imported energy on growth patterns and domestic prices, the implications of commoditization of traditional energy sources (e.g., the collapse of wood as "free good" and the transition to charcoal), and the role of government energy policy actions in development planning through investment, regulation, subsidization, pricing, marketing.

In the end, few general hypotheses on the energy/development dynamic offer useful guidance in the context of the particular economic trajectory, institutions, and resources of a given country. The proper assessment of energy problems and alternatives requires country-specific detail on current and forecast end-use consumption, supply and conversion pathways, and ecological and land-use patterns. Only in a detailed planning framework can the complex connections between development and energy be clarified. And, only then can planners ensure that development targets are consistent with energy constraints and conversely that timely energy policy initiatives permit the achievement of economic and social goals.

The Kenyan Economy

In the years since independence, Kenya has made significant advances in economic and social development. Both the needs and the opportunity for substantial further progress now exist. The recent history of development has prepared the way for a transition to this new phase. At the same time, aspects of this very development, and of the international economic context, put constraints on achieving such a transition.

Energy-related issues are significant here. As the modern sector has grown, so too have commercial energy requirements, particularly for oil, with severe consequences for the balance of payments as oil prices have increased dramatically. Similarly, the cost of other imports required for development, including machinery and transport equipment and intermediate goods, have also been rising during this period, and are expected to do so (5,6,7). On the other hand, increasing quantities of energy and capital inputs are important components of development. Additionally, a rapid annual rate of urbanization, close to 7 per cent in the last decade, poses some problems and challenges in Kenya where stabilization and diversification of the rural economy, expanded food production, and improved conditions of life for the rural population are desired. Here, too, more energy and capital investments may be required.

The performance of the Kenyan economy can be summarized by examining the behaviour of some of the quantitative development indicators during the post-independence era. The real annual

growth rate in GDP averaged 5.8 per cent during this period, with
however, substantial variations (6.4 per cent from 1964 to 1972,
and 4.7 per cent from 1972 to 1977) (8). At the same time
population increased at a rate of about 3.9 per cent. Thus, two
indicators of development, growth of absolute real GDP (that is,
domestic output of goods and services) and growth of real GDP per
capita (about 1.9 per cent from 1964-78), were at reasonably
healthy levels during the course of this period. Fluctuations,
arising from for example sharp rises or declines in export
commodities prices, from adverse weather conditions, or from
stagnation in the international economy, are difficult to avoid,
but could be ameliorated by further development and
diversification of the economy. Despite some setbacks and
slowdown since the mid 1970's, the overall achievement has been
substantial.

The tables below summarize the overall economic growth in
Kenya from 1970 to 1979 as well as some of the structure of that
growth. (All figures are calculated to inform energy accounts for
a base year of 1980). As indicated in Table 2.1, real GDP has
grown at an average annual rate of 4.9 per cent since 1970. In
current prices most sectors' contribution to GDP grew at
substantial rates - 9-17% per year (see Table 2.2) (9).

The value of both imports and exports has increased fourfold
during the 1970-79 period, and thus the trade balance deficit has
also increased by this amount, from K£ 49.2 million to K£ 206.9
million (see Table 2.3 for summary statistics). One major
component of this change has been fuel and lubricants imports,
which have increased tenfold in value and from a tenth of total
imports in 1970 to a quarter in 1979. At the same time, key
debt-service indicators have remained relatively stable. Debt
services as a percentage of GNP changed from 2.6 per cent in 1970
to 2.4 per cent in 1978, and as a percentage of exports, from 7.9
per cent to 8.3 per cent (10).

Agriculture continues to be the dominant sector of the
economy, contributing more than one-third of total GDP and
employing more than three-quarters of Kenya's labour force. There
has not been any dramatic change in this over the last decade and
a half. However, the small declines in the fraction of the work
force occupied in agriculture have been accompanied by large
increases in the fractions in industry and services.

Other consequences of socio-economic development include
substantial improvement in the infrastructure, services and
industrial capacity of the nation, including road improvement and
extension, railway rolling-stock acquisition, pipeline, airport
and new hydro-electric facility construction, irrigation scheme
expansion, and additional schools, hospitals, and extension
services. A dramatic increase in the numbers of children
attending primary and secondary schools has occurred in the last
two decades. The percentage of the respective age groups enrolled
in schools has grown from 47 per cent in 1960 to about 100 per

- 13 -

Table 2.1

GDP GROWTH RATES, 1970-80

Year	GDP Growth Rate (Percent)	
	Current Prices	Constant* Prices
1970	9.7	6.8
1971	12.2	7.0
1972	13.8	6.8
1973	14.6	4.3
1974	18.9	1.1
1975	12.6	4.1
1976	20.8	2.4
1977	28.4	8.8
1978	10.5	6.6
1979	10.4	3.3
1980	12.6	3.0
Mean	15.0	4.9

Source: Schipper (Revised)   * Using GDP Deflator.

Table 2.2

GDP BY SOURCE, AT CURRENT PRICES

	KL(Millions)		Percent		1970-1980
	1970	1980	1970	1980	Growth Rate pa
Agriculture, Forestry and Fishing	173.0	723.7	33.1	32.5	15.4
Mining and Quarrying	2.4	5.7	0.5	0.3	9.0
Manufacturing	62.2	295.1	11.9	13.2	16.8
Electricity & Water	12.0	47.6	2.3	2.1	14.8
Construction	62.4	137.9	5.1	6.2	8.3
Wholesale & Retail Trade, Hotels & Restaurants	55.8	244.7	10.7	11.0	15.9
Transport & Communication	40.8	127.8	7.8	5.7	12.1
Government Services	76.5	332.4	14.7	14.9	15.8
Other Services	72.8	299.6	13.9	13.4	15.2
Total GDP	557.9	2,214.5	100.0	100.0	15.6

Source: Schipper (Revised)

Table 2.3

EXPORTS AND IMPORTS OF MAJOR PRODUCTS
KL(Millions)

	1970		1975		1977		1978		1979	
	Value	%	Value	%	Value	%	Value	%	Value	%
Petroleum-product Exports	12.3	11.9	48.7	21.1	72.4	14.7	60.3	15.9	68.0	17.3
Total Exports	108.8	100.0	238.0	100.0	501.8	100.0	395.7	100.0	412.8	100.0
Fuels and Lubri-cants Imports	14.8	9.4	95.8	26.4	117.1	22.0	117.8	17.8	146.8	23.7
Total Imports	158.0	100.0	362.6	100.0	531.4	100.0	661.2	100.0	619.7	100.0
Trade Balance	-49.2		-124.6		-29.6		-265.5		-206.9	

cent in 1977 for primary schools, and 2 per cent in 1960 to 17 per cent in 1977 for secondary schools, while during this same period the adult literacy rate has increased from 20 per cent to 40 per cent. The number of nurses per capita has doubled from 1960 to 1977, and life expectancy has increased from 47 to 53 years.

The 1979-83 Development Plan outlines a number of key objectives for the Kenyan economy. Among these are increased and more equitable distribution of real income and improved conditions of life for the Kenyan people. A target of 6.3 per cent overall economic growth has been set. This is to be accompanied by a shift from the successful import substitution phase (from 1964 to the present), to a phase based upon expansion of exports. Given the constraints imposed by balance of payments deficits this will be difficult, especially since expansion requires increased fuel and capital inputs. Thus more efficient use of physical and monetary resources has been emphasized. Emphasis is also given to diversification and geographical dispersion of investment and therefore of development. Thus some attention will shift back from the earlier priority on urban infrastructure to rural infrastructure and institutions. Finally, the need to expand food production, as population expands by about 4 per cent per annum and increased nutritional levels are targeted, requires both expansion of agriculture into new lands and intensification through techniques such as double cropping and improved methods of cultivation. Increase in the productivity of land would likely require additional capital and other inputs such as fuels and fertilizer.

Integrated Energy Planning

The objective of energy planning assessment is to facilitate the achievement of near and long term economic and social development goals. Success in achieving these goals requires that energy resources of the proper type and magnitude be available to sustain the evolution of various sectors of society, and that cost-effective energy use pathways from resources and intermediate conversion to final demand be achieved.

All too often the development of an integrated energy planning process - one which can specify needs and establish timely programmes - has been evaluated on an aggregate basis or with respect to particular projects. The twin pitfalls for national energy planning of overgeneralization and overspecificity do not provide an adequate basis for concrete programmatic long-range planning. Aggregate representations do not provide sufficient detail to identify problems, constraints and opportunities to which policy initiatives can be addressed in a timely manner. A focus upon specific projects, sectors, or elements of the energy/development supply-demand picture does not take account of the variety of interactive effects and tradeoffs associated with energy-use and energy-policy options. Both approaches fail to address the energy and development issues in an integrated and systematic manner. Therefore, in addressing the problem of energy and development in a specific national context, the general issues discussed earlier must be represented analytically with sufficient detail, articulation, and comprehensiveness to allow for integrated energy, resource, and strategic economic planning.

The general requirements can be made more specific. First, development objectives embody economic and demographic futures with which energy constraints and requirements must be associated. These include sector-specific growth in output, energy intensiveness, and fuel mix. Changes in income distribution will also affect consumption patterns through technology and fuel choices. Moreover, expectations and objectives for the relative growth in traditional and modern sectors must be represented analytically in order to anticipate problems and formulate policy. Similarly, policy must be based upon sufficient information on a regional as well as national basis if local imbalances are to be identified and corrected. Futhermore, constraints on foreign exchange and labour require that energy supply/demand problems and policies be addressed in sufficient detail and articulation so that opportunities and constraints to developing indigenous resources, using local labour and manufacturing capacity, can be identified. The competing uses of land for food, exports, and fuel, each of which has energy and foreign exchange requirements and impacts must be adequately addressed in any attempt to develop an analytic framework for energy planning. Finally, the costs, benefits, foreign exchange and socio-economic aspects of energy policy options must be evaluated so that alternatives can be compared in a meaningful way.

Most of the requirements for energy planning dicussed above are embodied in the analyses undertaken for the Fuelwood Cycle project. The analytical tool developed for energy accounting and supply/demand analysis - the LDC Energy Alternatives Planning Model (LEAP) - provides the basis for representing the major economic, demographic, and physical interactions. In the chapters that follow these and related analyses are described and results presented and discussed.

CHAPTER 3 KENYA'S CURRENT ENERGY BALANCE

In this chapter we wish to document the existing flow
pattern of energy use in Kenya from sources through conversion
processes to the final point of consumption. The result is a
"snapshot" supply and demand relationship for 1980, the base year
used throughout this investigation. This picture, while helpful
in its own right in clarifying the current situation, serves as
the point of departure for the Base and Policy Case projections
developed in later chapters.

We summarize in the subsections below the findings on the
current energy flows, referring where relevant to the appropriate
technical volumes for more detailed description. In keeping with
its special focus in this study, the wood resource in Kenya is
discussed in its own chapter 4. Summary results are presented in
Table 3.1 below in the form of an energy balance sheet. This
traces the flow from primary energy resources (indigenous and
imported) through conversion losses, and exports (appearing as
negative consumption in the table) to final consumption. This
final consumption is in turn broken down further by key
sectoral/end-use components of demand.

As shown in Table 3.1, of the total annual primary energy
requirements (443.46 PJ), 74.3 per cent comes from non-commercial
sources (fuelwood and residues). Wood alone, including
commercially exploited wood resources for industrially related
purposes, comprises about three-quarters of the energy resource
base in Kenya.

The proportion of total final consumption accounted for by
wood is only 72 per cent, however. This reflects the large amount
of wood loss, about 84.38 PJ (per annum) or 19 per cent of total
energy requirements, in the conversion of wood to charcoal. The
composition of final (or end-use) consumption by major fuel types
is shown in Table 3.2 below. As indicated, petroleum products,
coal and electricity account for 27 per cent of total final
energy consumption (87.96 PJ). Of this quantity, the bulk, 93 per
cent is met by petroleum products.

Detailed discussion of current final consumption,
conversion, processes, and energy resources are the subjects,
respectively, of the next three sections.

End-Use Approach

The demand side analysis employed an "end-use" approach. It
is based on the principle of disaggregation wherein energy
requirements at the point of consumption are used as the analytic
building blocks. Such an approach permits demand projections and
provides a clear quantitative framework for evaluating the
potential for and costs of alternative policy options by tracking

Table 3.1

1980 KENYA ENERGY BALANCE: (Million Giga-Joules)

	Coal	Crude	Petroleum Products	Hydro*	Geo-thermal	Elec-tricity	Ind.Wood	Total Commercial	Fuelwood	Charcoal	Biomass/Residue	Total Non-Commercial	Grand Total
Indigenous	0.00	0.00	0.00	3.96	0.00	0.00	12.54	16.50	320.17	0.00	9.31	329.48	345.98
Imports	1.38	127.60	9.26	0.00	0.00	1.20	0.00	139.44	0.00	0.00	0.00	0.00	139.44
Exports	0.00	0.00	-41.96	0.00	0.00	0.00	0.00	-41.96	0.00	0.00	0.00	0.00	-41.96
Total Requirements	1.38	127.60	-32.70	3.96	0.00	1.20	12.54	113.98	320.17	0.00	9.31	329.48	443.46
Dist.Loss	-0.07	0.00	-4.25	0.00	0.00	-0.79	0.00	-5.11	-10.71	-1.33	-0.32	-12.36	-17.48
Elec.Generation	0.00	0.00	-5.98	-3.96	0.00	5.41	0.00	-4.53	0.00	0.00	0.00	0.00	-4.53
Refineries	0.00	-127.60	123.78	0.00	0.00	0.00	0.00	-3.83	0.00	0.00	0.00	0.00	-3.83
Charcoal Prod.	0.00	0.00	0.00	0.00	0.00	0.00	0.00	0.00	-111.03	26.65	0.00	-84.38	-84.38
Mill and Harvest	0.00	0.00	0.00	0.00	0.00	0.00	-6.24	-6.24	4.99	0.00	0.00	4.99	-1.25
Total Final Consumption	1.31	0.00	80.84	0.00	0.00	5.81	6.30	94.26	203.43	25.31	8.98	237.72	331.99
Urban Households	-	-	3.68	-	-	2.08	-	5.76	3.03	12.66	-	15.69	21.45
Cooking/Heating	-	-	1.96	-	-	.74	-	2.70	3.03	11.00	-	14.03	16.73
Lighting	-	-	1.73	-	-	.48	-	2.21	-	-	-	-	2.21
Other	-	-	-	-	-	.86	-	.86	-	1.66	-	1.66	2.52
Rural Households	-	-	4.19	-	-	-	-	4.19	150.56	9.25	8.98	168.79	172.98
Cooking/Heating	-	-	.51	-	-	-	-	.51	150.56	9.25	8.98	168.79	169.30
Lighting	-	-	3.68	-	-	-	-	3.68	-	-	-	-	3.68
Agriculture	-	-	7.64	-	-	.59	-	8.23	-	-	-	-	8.23
Industry	1.31	-	19.08	-	-	1.79	6.30	28.48	48.24	3.02	-	51.26	79.74
Large	1.31	-	19.00	-	-	1.77	6.30	28.38	17.44	-	-	17.44	45.82
Informal Urban	-	-	.08	-	-	.02	-	.10	.39	.95	-	1.34	1.44
Informal Rural	-	-	-	-	-	-	-	-	30.41	2.07	-	32.48	32.48
Commercial	-	-	.91	-	-	1.31	-	2.22	1.60	-	-	1.99	4.21
Schools/Hospitals	-	-	.28	-	-	.13	-	.41	1.60	-	-	1.99	2.40
Offices	-	-	.13	-	-	.78	-	.91	-	-	-	-	.91
Hotels	-	-	.51	-	-	.16	-	.66	-	-	-	-	.66
Small	-	-	-	-	-	.24	-	.24	-	-	-	-	.24
Transportation	-	-	45.33	-	-	.05	-	45.38	-	-	-	-	45.38
Road	-	-	29.73	-	-	-	-	29.73	-	-	-	-	29.73
Rail	-	-	2.52	-	-	-	-	2.52	-	-	-	-	2.52
Air	-	-	11.89	-	-	-	-	11.89	-	-	-	-	11.89
Other	-	-	1.18	-	-	.05	-	1.23	-	-	-	-	1.23

* Efficiency taken at one. (This analysis excludes bagasse, which accounts for 5.6 million GJ in industry).

Table 3.2

1980 ENERGY FOR FINAL DEMAND: PERCENTAGE BREAKDOWNS (million GJ)

	Commercial	%	Non-Commercial	%	Total	%
Electricity	5.81	6	-	-	5.81	2
Petro.Products						
Plus Coal	82.15	87	-	-	82.15	25
Charcoal	-	-	25.31	11	25.31	8
Fuelwood	-	-	203.43	85	203.43	60
Crop Residue	-	-	8.98	4	8.98	3
Industrial Wood	6.30	7	-	-	6.30	2
	94.26	100%	237.72	100%	331.99	100%
Total	28%		72%		100%	

impacts at the level of user equipment and behaviour adjustments. Further, the concrete relationship between economic goals, physical equipment stock, and energy requirements can be specified. Finally, appropriate timeframes for effective phase-in of demand management policy options (e.g., fuel switching, efficiency improvement, pricing policy) and supply enhancement strategies can be evaluated. (For more detail, see volume 9 cited in Table 1.1)

The end-use approach can be contrasted with long-range aggregate projections of energy. Projections based on time trending of summary energy statistics or global historic relationships between economic variables and energy demand can be misleading and not allow for policy assessment at an adequate level of detail. Making projections based on historic relationships has been likened to attempting to drive forward by looking through a rearview mirror.

The goal of disaggregating of demand at the point of end-use is limited by the availablity and quality of data to characterize the type and quantity of the major categories of energy-using stock and their usage levels. A good deal of research and survey effort went into supplementing the existing data base for Kenya.(For more detail, see volume 1-8 cited in Table 1.1) The degree of disaggregation which the data supports at this time and which was used in this exploration, is summarized in Table 3.3. Moreover, these sector/subsector/end-use combinations are disaggregated one step further into device and fuel combinations; for example, cooking may be undertaken on electric stoves, charcoal jiko etc. Finally, end-use demand depends upon consumption patterns which may differ for social and economic reasons, e.g. between urban and rural households and at various income levels.

After summarizing the end-use consumption estimates below, the remainder of this subsection is devoted to brief sector-by sector dicussions of the results. Further explication of data, methodology, and detailed computer outputs are deferred to the volume on Energy Planning in Developing Countries.

Summary Demand Characteristics

As reported in Table 3.1 above, final consumption of energy at the end-use was about 331.99 PJ in 1980. This excludes, it will be recalled, the 111.47 PJ of energy consumption in the energy sector itself (charcoal production, electrical generation, and fuel refining) as well as losses incurred in the distribution of fuel to the point of consumption. The structure of the end-use demand is revealed in Table 3.4 below which gives estimates of the 1980 percentage composition of demand by major sector and fuel types. We shall have occasion below, in the detailed discussion of sectoral demand characteristics, to refer to this

Table 3.3

END-USE CATEGORIES EMPLOYED

Sector	Subsector	End-Use +
Urban Household	5 Income Groups	Cooking/Water Heating Space Heating Lighting Refrigeration Miscellaneous
Rural Household	3 Income Groups	Cooking/Water Heating Space Heating Lighting Miscellaneous
Agriculture	*	*
Informal Industry Urban	(4 Categories)	Lighting Process Heat Cooking Washing Motor Drive Miscellaneous
Informal Industry Rural	(8 Categories)	*
Large Industry	(11 Categories)	*
Transportation	Private Passenger Public Passenger Rail Air Pipeline Steamship	Auto, Pickups Trucks, Buses, Minibuses Passenger, Freight Commercial, Other Pumping Commercial
Tertiary	Schools/Hospitals Offices Hotels Small Consumers	*

+ Each end-use broken down by appropriate device and fuel combinations.

* Current data availability did not support further disaggregation.

Table 3.4

COMPOSITION OF END-USE CONSUMPTION BY SECTOR AND MAIN FUEL TYPE

Sector	Wood (63%)	Charcoal (8%)	Residue (3%)	Petroleum Products (24%)	Electricity (2%)	Total (100%)
Urban HH	1%	50%	-	5%	36%	6%
Rural HH	72	37	100	5	-	53
Agriculture	-	-	-	9	10	2
Industry	26	12	-	24	31	24
Commercial	1	1	-	1	22	1
Transportation	-	-	-	56	1	14
	100%	100%	100%	100%	100%	100%

structure. The variation in sectoral portions of fuel demands is particularly noteworthy in providing an initial roadmap for policy attention.

Urban Household Sector

In 1980, end-uses associated with the urban domestic sector consumed 21.45 million gigajoules of energy, roughly 6 per cent of total final energy consumption in Kenya. Charcoal consumption within this sector amounts to 50 per cent of the national total. Thus, in designing a framework for fuelwood policy, the urban household sector warrants particular attention. While this sector at present does not account for a major absolute share of energy requirements, its significance for energy planning is greater than its present dimensions would suggest. Energy use within this sector is expected to grow rapidly due primarily to a pattern of significant migration from the rural areas to the cities (Chapter 5). Much of the present urban population, for example, consists of recent migrants.

Aside from insuring greater quantitative significance for this sector, the phenomenon of migration from countryside to city has a number of qualitative consequences in regard to energy use among urban households. Firstly, the mass influx of population from low income areas in the countryside implies that many urban households will initially be in a relatively weak economic condition. Secondly, they will be inclined toward energy modes associated with their earlier practices and customs. These consequences are indeed borne out by the current research. For example, project surveys show that wood consumption directly as wood fuel is a significant contributor to total energy use among low income urban households (see Table 3.5 for income categories). In fact, the urban energy consumption of the lowest income households is almost entirely wood based, much of it in the form of charcoal. This pattern presumably has become more pronounced as a consequence of the rise in the price of kerosene relative to charcoal and resulting substitution effects.

At the same time, those urban households which become more thoroughly integrated into the commercial economy show marked qualitative changes in their patterns of energy usage. For instance, low to middle level urban households use kerosene for lighting and to a more limited degree for heating. The use of bottled gas also begins to emerge at middle income levels. Finally, with rising income, electricity is used for an increasing variety of purposes. Electricity among lower and middle income users is utilized mainly for lighting, displacing kerosene within that end-use category. More affluent households expand and vary their uses of electricity. Electricity is used by such families for cooking and refrigeration and, among the most affluent, for water and space heating, and to power miscellaneous consumer durables.

These observations are all reflected in our base year data for the urban household sector. The data were derived primarily from two surveys of a cross-section of urban households. The first survey was conducted in the primate city, Nairobi, the capital of Kenya. The second survey, based on an understanding of city rank-size relationship (excluding the primate city), surveyed a major urban centre, Mombasa, a frontier town, Isiolo and included such diverse regional environments as Machakos, Kisumu, and Meru. These surveys attempted, among other things, to identify the range of end-uses, energy modes, and fuel consumption rates for various urban households. The primary distinguishing characteristic among households is income. Households are divided into five major income classes as delineated in Table 3.5.

The analysis reveals the presence of a significant influence of income on energy demand, both in a qualitative and in a quantitative sense. Table 3.6 shows consumption of wood fuel, charcoal and electricity over all end-uses for each of the five income classes. Note the marked decrease in fuelwood, the more gradual decline in charcoal usage, and the rise in the use of electricity.

There are a number of implications of these observations for planners. Of primary interest is the long-known association between urbanization and charcoal use. Insofar as charcoal production involves the secondary conversion of wood, the continued migration from rural to urban areas in Kenya will exacerbate the fuelwood crisis considerably, in the absence of policies to improve the efficiencies of charcoal conversion processes. This is borne out in the energy use projections described later.

Of further consequence are certain negative feedback phenomena associated with economic development. As development proceeds and urban families experience increases in income, they are apt to switch from a wood based regime to an energy use pattern which emphasizes electricity and imported energy forms. The capital and foreign exchange requirements imposed by this transition can serve to inhibit the allocation of capital and foreign exchange for purposes of industrialization and expansion of infrastructures and services, retarding the development process, if foreign exchange holdings remain static. In reality, industrialization and the growth of the modern sector proceed apace, as does the consumption of modern fuel by the urban population. The demand for modern fuel propels the development of the energy sector (e.g. electricity and mining). But to understand this demand, the income etc. the income elasticity aspects of urban household energy use are of central importance.

Table 3.5

INCOME GROUP CATEGORIES

Income Group	1980 KSh per Annum
1	0 - 3,092
2	3,093 - 9,108
3	9,109 - 18,216
4	18,217 - 54,648
5	54,649 -

Rural Domestic Sector

Kenya is still a predominantly rural country. In 1980, eighty-five percent of the total population was rural (see Chapter 5). Further, 1980 energy consumption in Kenya originating in the rural household sector equalled 173 million gigajoules. This, as we have seen in Table 3.4, is more than half of total resource end-use consumption, a level considerably greater than that of any other sector. Moreover, this sector accounted for 15 million gigajoules of final fuelwood consumption, or about three-quarters of the national total. Even charcoal consumption in this sector at 9.25 million gigajoules is 36 per cent of total charcoal consumption, a somewhat unanticipated result.

Clearly, then, the formulation of energy policy for the short and medium range future must take close account of the dynamics of the rural household sector. The current study acknowledged the central importance of the sector by conducting an extensive energy-use survey of rural households in conjunction with the Kenyan Central Bureau of Statistics. This is described in detail in the volume on rural household energy consumption. Through the survey, the major energy-use patterns among rural households were identified. In particular, it was discovered that regardless of income class, biomass constitutes the overwhelming basis for rural energy consumption. Electricity does not occur as a significant factor primarily because of limitations in the extent of the distribution grid. Kerosene accounts for only 3.7 million gigajoules in the sector, or 1 per cent of demand. The rural household sector is by and large preindustrial in its energy-use patterns.

A further observation of consequence emerges upon examination of the end-use breakdown within this sector. Cooking emerges as the overwhelming end-use allocation of energy, accounting for 169 million gigajoules, or 98 per cent of demand. Lighting, the other end-use reported by a significant number of households, accounts for the remainder.

Table 3.6

1980 URBAN ENERGY CONSUMPTION BY INCOME CLASS (million gigajoules)

Income Group	Households (Millions)	% Households	Fuelwood	Charcoal	Kerosene	Electricity	Bottled Gas
1	.03	5	.58	.29	.08	-	-
2	.13	23	1.07	2.69	.74	-	-
3	.15	26	.89	3.86	.91	.07	.06
4	.20	34	.44	4.81	1.04	.62	.45
5	.07	12	.05	1.01	.12	1.39	.28
All	.58	100%	3.03	12.66	2.89	2.08	.79

The policy implications of this situation are clear. Reduction in the demand for fuelwood can be effected either through improvements in the end-use efficiency of rural cooking or through switching of fuels at the end-use. The latter could be achieved in principle, for example, by extending the central electricity grid, promoting decentralized technologies relying on indigenous sources of energy such as mini-hydro, solar, photovoltaic, biogas, wind, etc., or by the introduction of "horizontal" technologies (e.g. maize milling) that would reduce the energy required for food preparation. We shall see, however, that fuel switching to electricity exacerbates the modern sector problems of oil dependence and capital investment constraints. And there is every indication that electricity, in the next couple of generations, would not be a primary fuel for cooking.

Consumption per household for cooking occurs in a range of 62-69 gigajoules over all three income classes considered. The rural household sector, therefore, offers in a sense a fortunate concentration of energy expenditure in a single mode and end-use. The problem is straightforward, to identify and account for much of the overall national consumption. Currently, energy requirement in this section is largely independent of the vicissitudes of commercial and economic factors such as price and income.

Agriculture

It is an apparent irony that, while agriculture is the major occupation of the working population, commercial energy consumption in the agricultural sector (8.2 million gigajoules) amounts only to 2.5 per cent of total energy consumption in Kenya. This is about 6.0 per cent of final demand for non-household consumption. The relatively low proportion of agriculture in overall energy use is a function of several factors, the most notable of which is that agriculture in Kenya relies to a significant degree on human and animal draught power and on direct solar power for the drying of crops. None of these energy sources is accounted directly in our analysis as a basis for energy use.

The composition of commercial fuels employed in the agricultural sector reflects mainly the use of tractors and other farm machinery in large commercial farms. Diesel fuel comprises eighty percent of all commercial energy employed in agriculture. About 12 per cent is gasoline and 7 per cent electricity.

Aside from solar and animate forms of energy, which are not included in the above figures, additional non-commercial energy is consumed in the processing (e.g. drying and curing) of some agricultural products. In particular about 17.4 million gigajoules of wood are consumed in the larger tea, tobacco and sugar industries, and in addition about 35 million gigajoules of wood are consumed for agricultural drying and tobacco curing in rural cottage industry. These additional categories are treated separately in the following section. Quite clearly, they add substantially to non-household rural energy use.

Industry

The importance of the large industrial sector lies not so much in the absolute demand for energy originating in this sector, but rather in its reliance on commercial fuels. Large industry accounts for 18 per cent of total energy consumption in Kenya, but 23 per cent of the demand for petroleum products and 31 per cent of the demand for electricity (see Table 3.1). The economical use of petroleum imports would thus be facilitated by a more efficient pattern of energy use by large industrial firms. At the same time, large industry offers scope for the conservation of imported oil through fuel switching away from oil and toward biomass and non-oil generated electricity. We shall return to these possibilities in chapters 6 and 7.

The magnitude of energy use among different industries is highly variable. Generally speaking, in Kenya, the more energy intensive sectors account for a small proportion of total industrial activity and show slower growth than sectors which are less energy intensive as shown in Table 3.7. Note that non-metallic materials and clay and glass rank last in both their current activity levels and in their growth rates, but first in energy intensiveness.

In addition to the primarily urban, modern industrial sectors described above, a complete national energy demand accounting must include fuel use in other industries located primarily in rural areas. This is especially important for the present study since these industries depend on wood as their principal energy resource. The fuelwood demand in this industrial sub-sector occurs in industries associated with agricultural processing (drying and curing for tea, tobacco, and sugar) in rural wood processing, in the use of wattle for tanning, and in pottery/brick, and baking facilities.

Estimates of current annual fuelwood use in these industries have been made on the basis of research undertaken by Mungale (11), Akinga (12), and Openshaw (13). These estimates appear in Table 3.8.

Average annual consumption of wood in these industries is about 1.08 million tonnes (17.2 PJ). This is about 8 per cent of total fuelwood consumption nationally.

Bagasse (sugar cane waste) accounts for about 12 per cent of industrial energy (5.6 PJ). It is used exclusively by the sugar industry in the process of sugar refining and supplying electricity to the sugar estates. At present an estimated 10 per cent of bagasse is wasted and it could be used to supply electricity to the grid system if agreement could be reached between the sugar companies and government.

Table 3.7

ENERGY INTENSITIES FOR SELECTED LARGE INDUSTRY SECTORS

Sector	1979 GDP (10^6 K£)	Growth Rate 1977/79	(Energy Intensity) GJ/1000 K£ Output	
			Oil	Electricity
Food	54.06	13	59.5	9.9
Textiles	11.79	22	114.8	24.6
Paper	6.06	33	279.0	13.7
Non-Metallic Materials	4.7	-2	1185.1	26.4
Clay & Glass	0.62	11	1280.3	49.4
Chemicals	5.01	43	167.2	14.1

Table 3.8

OTHER INDUSTRIAL WOOD REQUIREMENTS

Industry	Annual Wood Consumption (1000 Tonnes)	Annual Wood Consumption (GJ/Capital)
Tea	220-330 (275 Avg.)	.22-.33 (.28 Avg.)
Tobacco	80	.08
Sugar	50	.05
Wood Processing	300	.30
Wattle	40	.04
Pottery/Brick	30	.03
Baking	300	.30
Total Fuelwood	1020-1130 (1075 Avg.)	1.02-1.13 (1.08 Avg.)

Urban Informal Industry

The "informal industry" sector is found throughout urban Kenya. The sector includes such economic endeavors as small textile and apparel workshops, garages, furniture makers, restaurants, and the like. As a group, they are distinguished from the large industrial and commercial categories by their small scale and pre-modern technological and management character. The vast majority of these establishments carry on their operations without substantial use of modern sector fuels. Nonetheless, because informal industrial establishments are so widespread, it was deemed useful to study the pattern of informal urban industry energy use, especially demands for fuelwood and charcoal. This issue was researched through an extensive survey of informal industrial firms in Nairobi and Meru which is described in detail in volume 7.

The choice of those two urban areas was informed by the following methodological consideration. We sought to explore the hypothesis that the informal industry sector shows uniform patterns of energy use despite the size of city in which the establishment is located. For this purpose we chose two cities, one a major metropolis and the second a moderate sized town. Were the responses to our survey indicative of substantial differences in energy consumption patterns between the two cities, we would have undertaken additional research to ascertain energy use patterns throughout the urban hierarchy. However, our survey indicated that energy use in informal industry is indeed independent of urban population. Given this apparent invariance - and the small role of informal industry on national aggregate consumption - this research sufficed to allow generalisation to national level.

What the survey shows overall is that informal industry is inconsequential as a user of traditional fuels and consumes very little electricity or hydrocarbon fuels. The technologies associated with this sector are highly labour intensive. Informal urban industry accounts for but 0.4 per cent of total end-use energy consumption and 0.6 per cent of wood and charcoal consumption. Most of the fuelwood use originates in the food and drink sub-sector, primarily restaurants using charcoal for cooking. Thus, 87 per cent of the fuelwood used in informal urban industry occurs in the food and drink subsector. Workshops by contrast account for only 7 per cent.

The data on energy consumption per establishment type developed through the two-city survey were employed to generate a nationwide estimate by multiplication with the number of such establishments undertaken by the Central Bureau of Statistics. The basic end-use data are summarized in Table 3.9.

Table 3.9

1980 URBAN INFORMAL END-USE ASSUMPTIONS (PJ)

Subsector	$ Firms	End-Use (% with end-use)	Fuel Split	Intensity (GJ/firm)*
Clothing Personal	5400	Lighting (21%)	40% Kerosene	6.5
			60% electricity	3.6
		Process Heat (31%)	75% charcoal	17.8
			25% electricity	5.4
		Cooking (17%)	50% kerosene	4.3
			50% charcoal	2.4
		Washing (17%)	40% kerosene	1.4
			60% petrol	1.5
Garages/Mechanics	1990	Lighting (41%)	15% kerosene	1.5
			85% electricity	2.2
		Process Heat (66%)	19% charcoal	2.5
			19% kerosene	17.0
			38% petrol	0.4
			52% electricity	6.9
		Cooking (22%)	86% charcoal	10.1
			29% kerosene	3.4
		Washing (41%)	85% kerosene	31.7
			62% petrol	8.0
			15% diesel	29.2
		Motor Drive (41%)	46% petrol	12.8
			54% electricity	6.9
Food/Drink	4110	Lighting (77%)	91% kerosene	7.5
			13% electricity	3.9
		Process Heat (92%)	12% wood	452.5
			89% charcoal	139.3
			4% kerosene	14.8
		Cooking (98%)	20% wood	214.7
			94% charcoal	105.9
		Space Heat (8%)	43% wood	82.4
			57% charcoal	30.1
Workshop	1720	Lighting (44%)	58% kerosene	4.8
			42% electricity	1.7
		Process Heat (56%)	4% wood	9.3
			32% charcoal	118.7
			16% kerosene	28.0
			60% electricity	6.7
		Cooking (27%)	8% wood	9.3
			85% charcoal	13.5
			23% kerosene	2.7
		Paint Mixing (17%)	100% kerosene	6.7
		Motor Drive (27%)	100% electricity	6.9
		Washing (13%)	100% kerosene	1.2
		Space Heat (6%)	50% wood	9.3
			50% charcoal	10.2

* Average energy consumption per end-use/fuel combination among firms in subsector using that combination.

Rural Informal Industry

The informal rural industry sector includes two categories of demand, cottage industry and rural services. (This discussion excludes the demand for wood as construction material although this topic is covered in chapter 4).
Significant energy demand, in particular for fuelwood and charcoal, occurs in the rural informal or cottage industries. These industries are quite diverse, including brewing, pottery and brick making, blacksmiths, agricultural drying, fish curing, tobacco, butcheries, baking and eating places. Estimates have been made of annual fuel demands in each of these industries. These estimates are provided in Table 3.10.
The average annual consumption of fuelwood and charcoal in these industries is 2.66 GJ per capita for wood and .15 GJ per capita for charcoal. Most of the rural service requirements (e.g., hospitals and schools) are included under the "commercial" sector designation.

Commercial Institutional

This sector includes a number of energy using activities including schools, hospitals, office buildings, and hotels. It includes also a category of "small consumers", which reflects commercial accounts with East Africa Power and Light, which are too small to be accounted as large industry and too large to be accounted as informal industry. All in all, the commercial sector embraces 1.3 per cent of total end-use energy demand within Kenya.
In spite of its relatively small magnitude as an element in overall energy use, the commercial sector shows some interesting properties which deserve mention. For example, a high proportion of schools in Kenya are rural-based boarding schools, largely inaccessible to such commercial energy sources as electricity. Woodfuel, and to a lesser extent charcoal, are employed in such schools as primary fuels. For this reason wood-based fuels amount to 83 per cent of total consumption in the schools sub-sector.
Tourism is a major source of foreign exchange earnings in Kenya, growing at an annual rate of 7 per cent between 1968-75. Indeed the 1979-1983 Development Plan states that every effort will be made to increase the contribution of tourism and wildlife to foreign exchange earnings. While the absolute magnitude of tourism's contribution to energy use is not large, we shall see that its orientation toward commercial fuels offers some scope for cost-effective conservation measures (Chapter 6).
Office buildings and services are even more important as an originating end-use insofar as they account for almost twenty per cent of total electricity consumption. Here too the potential for conservation, e.g., through more efficient water heating installations, is promising.

Table 3.10

RURAL COTTAGE INDUSTRY DEMAND (1980)

Industry	Annual Consumption (1000 tonnes)		Annual Consumption (GJ per capita rural)	
	Wood	Charcoal	Wood	Charcoal
Brewing	900	-	1.07	-
Pottery/Brick	50	-	.06	-
Blacksmiths	-	23 (200 Wood)	-	.06
Agric. Drying	30	-	.04	-
Fish Curing	20	-	.02	-
Tobacco	30	-	.04	-
Butchers	200	23 (200 Wood)	.24	.06
Baking	110	-	.13	-
Eating Places	140	16 (140 Wood)	.17	.04
Poles	420	-	.50	-
Total	1900	62 (540 Wood)	2.27	.15

The 1980 breakdowns are displayed in Table 3.11.

Table 3.11

1980 COMMERCIAL/INSTITUTIONAL CONSUMPTION
(PJ)

Schools/Hospitals	2.39
Woodfuel	1.60
Charcoal	0.39
Bottled Gas	0.07
Kerosene	0.03
Residual Oil	0.17
Electricity	0.13
Solar	0.00
Offices/Other SE	0.92
Bottled Gas	0.04
Kerosene	0.01
Residual Oil	0.08
Electricity	0.78
Solar	0.00
Hotels	0.67
Bottled Gas	0.14
Kerosene	0.06
Residual Oil	0.32
Electricity	0.16
Solar	0.00
Wood/Charcoal	-
Small Consumers	0.24
Electricity	0.24
Total	4.21

Transportation

The transportation sector in Kenya is a significant user of energy. Total 1980 consumption originating in this sector amounted to 45.38 million gigajoules, or 13.7 per cent of final consumption. Consumption by the transportation sector is an important component of commercial fuel requirements. Of the 13.4 million barrels of oil consumed within Kenya in 1980, 6.0 million barrels originated in the transport sector. Of the remaining uses only the modern industrial sector proved a significant user of petroleum products at 3.4 million barrels, and 1.4 million barrels are used in refining the crude oil. Household consumption, largely in the form of kerosene for lighting, amounted to only 8 per cent of total consumption. Thus, it is fair to say that oil-import burdens in Kenya are largely a problem of transport demand.

The Kenyan transport sector is almost entirely a user of liquid, petroleum based fuels. Only in the transport of oil via pipeline is there evidence of significant electricity use, for example. It should be noted, however, that only inanimate sources of energy have been considered here. Animal and human power for transport are important additional sources.

Mechanized transport activity in Kenya, though petroleum based, uses highly diverse forms including gasoline, diesel, residual oil, and jet fuel. Consumption, moreover, is distributed among a wide variety of end-uses, as shown in Table 3.12.

Conversions

There are three important intermediate energy conversion processes in Kenya at this time. They are, respectively, the conversion of wood to charcoal, the conversion of crude oil to refined petroleum products, and the conversion of various primary energy forms in the generation of electricity. These are dicussed below in turn.

Charcoal Production

Of the 20.0 million tonnes of wood fuel consumed in Kenya in 1980, 7.3 million tonnes were converted to charcoal, and the remaining 12.7 million tonnes was burnt directly as fuel. Virtually all of the charcoal consumed in Kenya was produced in traditional earthen kilns at a relatively low efficiency. However, the relative wasteful earth kiln production methods are the only appropriate methods for many savannah areas where the cost of transporting wood to efficient modern kilns or transporting modern, mobile kilns to the wood is prohibitive. The 7.3 million tonnes of primary wood resource was converted to about 0.7 million tonnes of charcoal, thus there appears to be a substantial energy loss. Indeed, if wood was burnt directly there would be an energy saving, but not as much as first appears.

First, the energy content of charcoal is about twice that of fuelwood (33.1 gigagoules versus 16 gigajoules per tonne). Thus, charcoal is more convenient to use and cheaper to transport be-cause of higher energy intensity per unit and lower water content. Second, the conversion efficiency of charcoal jiko is typically about twice that of traditional open fires in Kenya. Therefore, the apparent 10:1 ratio in favour of wood is reduced to 2.5:1 when these two factors are considered. This is illustrated in Fig. 3.1. and Fig. 3.2.

Table 3.12

DISTRIBUTION OF ENERGY CONSUMPTION AMONG ALTERNATIVE
TRANSPORT MODES WITHIN THE TRANSPORT SECTOR

Transport Mode	Energy Consumption (PJ)	Percent
Private Vehicles	16.62	36.6
Public Commercial Vehicles (Including Matatu)	13.11	28.9
Rail	2.52	5.6
Air	11.89*	26.2
Pipeline	0.05	0.1
Steamship	1.18	2.6
Total	45.38	100.0

*   Of which 10.7 PJ was used by international flights.

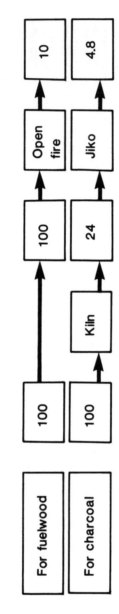

Figure 3.1 Overall Conversion – Fuelwood Versus Charcoal per Energy Unit

Figure 3.2 Translates the above conversion ratios and gives a wood fuel energy flow for Kenya

Figure 3.2 Wood Resource Energy Flows in Kenya, 1980 (millions of Gigajoules)

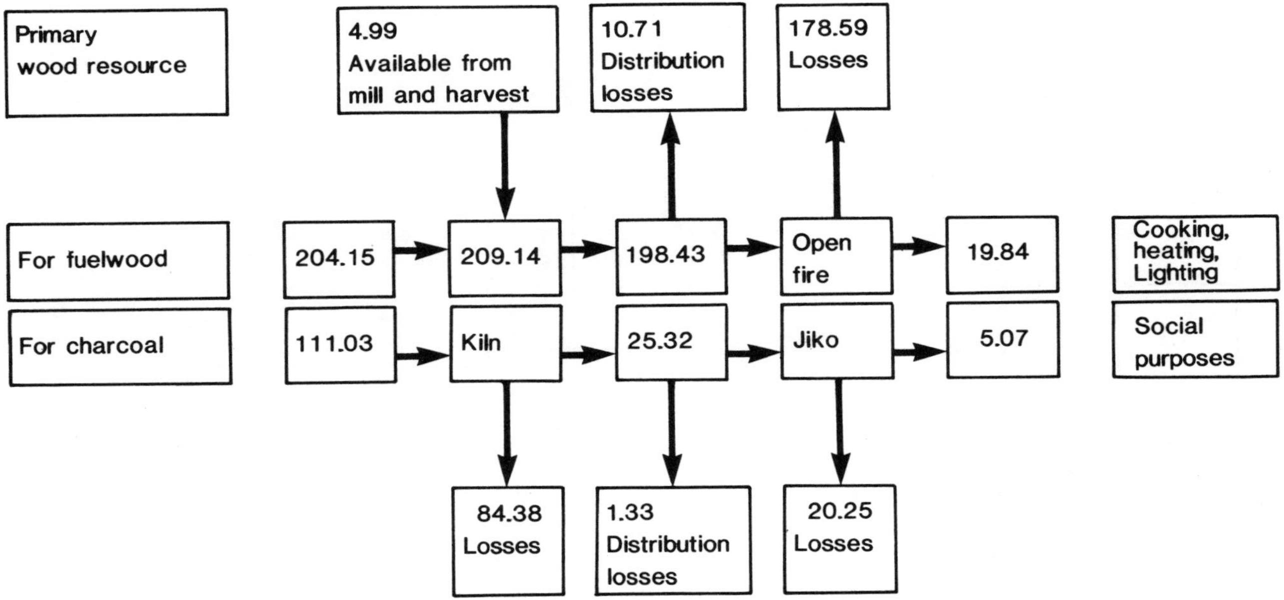

It can be seen, then, that under current conditions and practices charcoal use places a greater burden on wood resources than use of fuelwood for a given final demand serviced (i.e.about 2.5 to 1). Losses in the kiln conversion process figure prominently in this relative disadvantage.

Despite the observations made above, there are important reasons why charcoal remains an attractive fuel in Kenya and promises to increase in importance. These reasons are associated with cultural, economic, geographic and demographic factors. Charcoal usage in households is primarily an urban and higher income phenomenon. First, since the energy content of charcoal is about twice that of fuelwood per unit weight, convenience and economies in transport, storage and use make it desirable. Moreover, the higher efficiencies of jiko add to these economies. Urban areas are located along major transport routes so that a wider wood resource base (primarily in rangelands and savannah) may be drawn upon, benefitting from transport economies. Jiko use is considered a more convenient and attractive technology than simple wood burning and is generally an expression of income mobility. Finally, the commodity status of charcoal makes it an attractive option to entrepreneurs who can derive incomes from its production and distribution.

Fuelwood is the traditional energy source in rural Kenya for cooking, heating, lighting, social and ceremonial purposes. It is more readily accessible to the rural population for logistical and economic reasons. It has the advantage of providing light, along with other services, where electricity and kerosene are not available or affordable. On the other hand, as local sources are depleted, fuelwood use places increasing burdens on natural stocks of wood resources, household labour time budgets, and perhaps soil quality in areas where food production is carried out. However, compared to other energy forms the cooking devices have very low efficiencies and a little improvement both in fuelwood and charcoal stoves will save a considerable amount of energy.

Electricity Generation

Electrical energy utilization requires two distinct conversion processes. At the end-use, electricity drives a variety of equipment (motors, pumps, heaters, lightbulbs, communication devices, etc.).

The secondary conversion stage involves the use of some primary energy source such as oil or falling water to generate electricity. Energy losses occur at each of these two stages as well as in the transmission and distribution of electric power. Electricity generated by the combustion of primary fuel is less efficient than the direct use of that fuel due to these efficiency losses, in particular at the secondary conversion

stage where thermodynamic constraints limit practical conversion
efficiencies to about one-third (electrical energy out to primary
fuel in). However, electricity possesses some unique offsetting
advantages. It is energy of exceptionally high quality which can
be used as a source of both thermal and mechanical energy.
Primary fuels by contrast are often less versatile. For example,
falling water can be used as a mechanical source in the form of
water wheels, but not as a direct heat source; coal can be
easily burned for heat, but only with difficulty can it serve as
a source of mechanical energy in the form of a steam engine.
Steam engines are relatively cumbersome and unsuitable for many
mechanical applications. Indeed, the versatility of electricity
as a "motive force" is a primary reason why historically it has
been linked to industrializing and diversifying economies.
    Additionally, electricity generation permits the conversion
of highly specialized energy sources into a useful energy form.
The controlled fission reactor is not very useful as a direct
source of energy but widely used as an electricity source. Wind
power is harnessed usefully as an electricity generator.
Photoelectricity converts sunlight directly into electricity.
Even the energy of the ocean waves and of the tides can be
converted into electricity.
    The substantial advantages of electricity as an energy
source suggest that the electrification of Kenya should be a
significant priority in Kenya's medium term development strategy.
Electricity is a major factor in the expansion of industrial
activity. Furthermore, the natural endowment is weighted in
favour of energy goods which can best be utilized as a source of
electric power. Fossil fuels are entirely imported, while
hydro-electric power and geothermal resources are available
domestically.
    Hydroelectric resources are especially prominent in Kenya
relative to other sources of electrical generation. Total
hydroelectric planned potential is officially estimated at 1,115
MW, approximately three times existing electricity demand. Of
this potential, 295 MW is now installed and 820 MW is planned. At
present, all installed hydroelectric capacity is associated with
the Tana River watershed (see Table 3.13) encompassing four
separate facilities. Seventy per cent of planned hydroelectric
development will also tap Tana River water. All hydro
possibilities other than those shown in Table 3.13 are of small
size and of little consequence to the overall energy balance.
(See chapter 6 for more discussion on mini-hydro.) Another
indirect source of hydro power could be via interconnections with
neighbouring countries. Kenya presently obtains 30 MW from the
Uganda Electricity Board. Tanzania and the Sudan offer
potentially usable sites with likely export potential.
    Other than hydro power, a significant non-fossil source of
electrical energy in Kenya is geothermal power. Planned
developments of geothermal energy for electrical generation are

Table 3.13

HYDRO AND GEOTHERMAL RESOURCES (MW)

River	Location/Power Station	Installed Capacity	Planned Potential	Total Exploitable Potential
Tana	Tana/Wanjii	22		
	Kindaruma	44		
	Kamburu	84		
	Gitaru	145		
	Upper Reservoir (Mithinga)	-	40	
	Kiambere	-	140	
	Mutonga	-	70	
	Grand Falls	-	80	
	Karura	-	40	
	Adamson's Falls	-	50	
	Koreh	-	80	
	Usueni	-	60	
	Total Tana	295	560	835
Nzoia	Webuye Falls	-	10	
Yala	Kimundi Confluence	-	40	
Sondu	Sondu	-	60	
Arror	Kapsowar	-	20	
Turkwell	Turkwell Gorge	-	100	
	Total Other Rivers	-	230	230
Geothermal	Olkaria Valley	-	30	174
	Other Areas	-	0	326
	Total Geothermal	-	30	500
Total Power		295	820	1,565

limited to the Olkaria Vally sites where potential geothermal capacity is accounted as 500 MW. Another study identifies potential geothermal sites in the vicinity of Lakes Bogoria, Naivasha, Elementeita, Magadi and Baringo (14).

Current load characteristics of the electricity consuming market in Kenya, coupled with the low capacity factors of hydro installations due to erratic stream flow and siltation, imply the need for supplementing baseload and peaking installations as we shall see in chapter 5. These facilities presently employ exotic fossil fuels largely in the forms of paraffin, residual and distillate oils. Of primary importance in the present supply configuration is the oil-fired steam generator at Kipevu, Mombasa, rated at 93 MW. The location of this baseload facility on the coast of Mombasa yields economies of transport, as this facility is in the neighborhood of Kenya's only oil refinery. Other fossil-fired plant includes two units totaling 26 MW of gas turbine capacity and 23 MW of diesel units. One of the gas turbine units burns paraffin, rather than distillate.

Aside from their reliance on imported energy sources, the thermal generating facilities in Kenya are disadvantageous in that they are relatively inefficient in comparison to state-of-the-art models. The efficiencies of existing units in Kenya are summarized in Table 3.14. This is due in part to the older condition of many of these units which has resulted in considerable derating of capacity. The present ratio of effective year-long capacity to nominal capacity accounting for seasonal fluctuations in stream flow is about 35 per cent. This ratio could be improved if the watershed areas were protected from indiscriminate cultivation, and trees were protected and replanted. Conversely, if the trees are removed and the land cultivated, then the river flow may become very erratic. Table 3.15 summarizes the capacity and generation estimates for 1980 normalized to average conditions of stream flow, load shape and weather conditions.

Petroleum Production

The east African Oil Refinery began operations at Mombasa in 1964. The design capacity of the facility is 4.2 million tonnes per year of crude oil, though the achievable output appears to be around 3.6 million tonnes per year (15). To date, Kenya enjoys no indigenous production of crude oil. The quantity and value of imports have increased over time as shown for selected years in Table 3.17.(16) The price rises, of 1973 and 1979, are quite striking.

All of the crude oil processed in 1980 originated in the Middle East. The refinery system currently does not have the capability of transforming the heaviest components of this crude into the lighter petroleum products. The output mix is not matched to domestic demand in Kenya, as shown in Table 3.18.

Table 3.14

EFFICIENCIES OF EXISTING THERMAL GENERATING UNITS IN KENYA

Unit	Type	Rated Capacity	Fuel	Kg/Kwh	Thermal Efficiency
Kipevu	Oil-fired Steam	30 MW 33 MW	Residual Oil	.30	27.7%
Kipevu	Oil-fired Steam	12.5 MW (2)	Residual Oil	.39	21.3
Kipevu	Oil-fired Steam	5 MW (2)	Residual Oil	.51	16.3
Kipevu	Gas turbine	12.2 MW	Paraffin	.43	19.4
Nairobi	Gas turbine	15.7 MW	Distillate	.43	19.4
South	Diesel	30.1 MW 6 units	Distillate	.29	28.7

Table 3.15

1980 ELECTRIC GENERATION AND CAPACITY

	Capacity (MW)	Generation (10^6 KWH)
Uganda Imports	30	333
Hydro Power	300	1100
Combustion Turbine	22	26
Diesel	19	26
Oil Steam	93	349
Total	464	1835

Electric sales currently have the sectoral breakdowns shown in Table 3.16.

Table 3.16

1980 ELECTRIC ENERGY DEMANDS

Sector	Demand (10^6 KWH)	%
Urban Household	577.78	31%
Agriculture	163.89	9
Commercial	363.89	20
Industry	497.23	27
Transportation	13.89	1
Transmission and Distribution Losses	220.00	12
Total	1836.68	100%

Table 3.17

QUANTITY AND VALUE OF CRUDE OIL IMPORTS

Year	Quantity (Thousand Tonnes)	Value (Million K£)
1965	1851	9.1
1970	2206	11.0
1975	2825	86.8
1980	3038	281.7

Table 3.18

1980 MIX OF REFINERY OUTPUT AND DOMESTIC DEMAND

Product	Demand % Wt.	Output % Wt.
Gas Oil and Diesel Oil	27.6	20.7
Kerosene	26.2	14.8
Fuel Oil and Bitumen	24.8	49.2
Gasolines	19.6	14.5
LPG	1.8	0.8
Total	100.0	100.0

In essence, to meet kerosene and gas demand excess fuel oil
is produced. A better match could be achieved by introducing new
cracking units (either hydro cracking or the less expensive but
less effective thermal cracking) which would reduce the import
crude requirements.

Refinery output was supplemented in 1980 by a small quantity
of imported products, about 22.2 thousand tonnes of gasoline and
gasoil. The excess refinery products are in turn exported. The
balance is shown in Figure 3.3.

Energy Resources Supplied

The energy resources supplied to meet Kenya's energy demand
in our base year, 1980, are presented in Table 3.19.

Note that this accounting of energy resources excludes crude
oil imports required for re-exportation of refined oil products.
Only two sources of energy are significant today, oil and wood
which together comprise over 95 per cent of primary energy
requirements. As we shall see in chapter 5, the Base Case
projections show a growing dependence on these fuels over the
next two decades and, in the absence of policy action, serious
uncertainties regarding their sufficiency. First, however,
greater analytic detail is required on the wood resource itself
to better understand its regional, land use and supply
characteristics in Kenya today.

Figure 3.3 1980 Petroleum Balances – Thousand tonnes
Million barrels

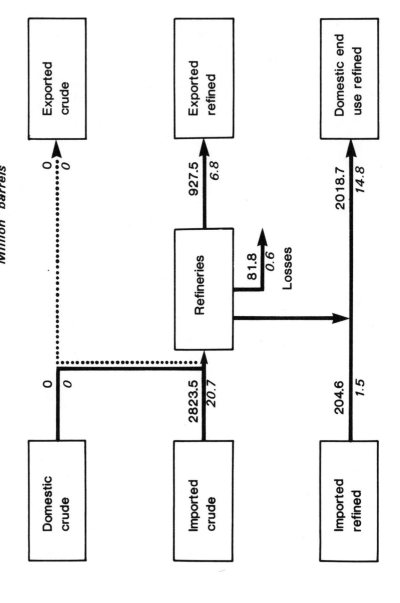

Table 3.19

ENERGY RESOURCES SUPPLIED

	Quantity (PJ)	%
Indigenous		
Wood	332.6	75.0
Hydro	4.0	0.9
Residues	9.3	2.1
Imports		
Crude Oil	85.6	19.3
Refined Oil	9.3	2.1
Coal	1.4	0.3
Electricity	1.2	0.3
Total	443.5	100.0%

CHAPTER 4. <u>WOOD RESOURCES AND AGRICULTURE</u>

Wood resources have traditionally played an important role for energy needs in early stages of national economic development. As development proceeds the emergence of more flexible solid and liquid fuels and electricity is expected to displace wood as the major primary energy resource. This is especially true in urban areas as industrial and commercial activity increases and standards of living rise, in rural areas as agriculture is modernized and scale economies are realized, and as transportation and other infrastructures and services are expanded. Unfortunately, as both the needs and costs for imported fuels have been escalating rapidly, continued pressure on wood resources has resulted. The problems that emerge include increased time allocated by rural households to fuelwood gathering, deforestation and the potential deterioration of soil conditions and agricultural productivity, and, in general, the potential for destabilization and devolution of the rural economy. At the center of this set of problems lies the competition between wood requirements and agricultural production requirements for scarce productive land. Thus, availability of and access to land for both wood resources and agricultural activity, and the ecological conditions governing both wood and agricultural output are critical aspects of the wood supply/demand picture in Kenya.

The present and future supply of wood resources in Kenya will depend on the interaction between wood demand, the stocks and yields of woody biomass, the competing uses of land, geographic factors influencing access to and transportability of woodfuels, and socio-economic factors such as access to tools, household labour economy and land tenure. These mutually conditioning factors determine the rate at which wood resources are drawn down. This is important since, due to the supply/demand interaction, wood is not a strictly renewable resource except under conditions of either natural abundance or wood management where supply is maintained above the levels of demands.

As has been shown, at present the demand for wood resources in Kenya dominates the overall energy requirements of the national economy. At the end-use level wood and charcoal requirements amount to more than 75 per cent of total demand. The wood component of primary energy resource requirements satisfies two major categories of demand. These are:

(1) Directly consumed as fuelwood, primarily in rural households and the rural economy.

(2) Consumed as charcoal after conversion in kilns, primarily in urban households.

In addition a third important use, especially in value added terms, is:

(3) Feedstock used in sawmills, paper and pulp mills, the panel industries, and industrial and rural construction.

A breakdown of estimated 1980 consumption is contained in Table 4.1.

Because of the nature of the supply/demand interaction for wood resources, it is necessary to make these distinctions (including a further distinction between industrial and rural construction) in order to allocate these demands properly to the appropriate ecological and geographical resource base. On the wood resource side, then, it is important to distinguish three levels in specifying available wood resources - geographic (i.e. regional), ecological, and land use category. On this basis wood production characteristics can then be specified in terms of stocks and annual yields of woody biomass, and other characteristics influencing the relationship between resources and both local and national demands.

Land Use

In specifying land use characteristics in Kenya, attention was given to geographical and ecological factors, competing functions, and socio-economic characteristics all of which affect the availability of wood resources. The land in Kenya was divided according to three hierarchical levels: provinces, ecological zones within provinces, and land-uses within each ecological zone. A description of the sources, methods, and results of these calculations is given in Volume 9.

Seven provinces were specified - Central/Nairobi, Coast, Eastern, Northeastern, Nyanza, Rift Valley, and Western provinces. While Kenya has great diversity in the ecological character of its land, due primarily to the wide range of altitudes and rainfall regimes throughout the country, it was convenient, based upon existing sources of data, to identify three broad ecological zones - High Potential, Medium Potential, Semi-Arid. These categories and estimated land areas are based primarily upon data from the Large Farm Survey, the Integrated Rural Survey, and the Kenya Rangeland Ecological Monitoring Unit (KREMU) land classification systems.

Table 4.2 provides the ecological zone breakdowns on a provincial and national basis. Note that on a national basis only about twenty per cent of land is high or medium potential. These are the lands upon which all agricultural production and all closed forests are primarily located. However, 70 per cent of tree resources are on the semi-arid lands. In addition, the high or medium potential land support the bulk of the population and a large part of national economic activity.

Table 4.1

1980 KENYA ESTIMATED WOOD CONSUMPTION

	Million Tonnes Roundwood Equivalent	%
Woodfuel	19.64	94%
Fuelwood	(12.83)	(61)
Charcoal	(6.81) *	(33)
Rural Poles	0.41	2
Industrial Wood	0.77 **	4
Total	20.82	100%

* Energy loss in conversion process is estimated at 5.18 million tonnes of wood equivalent.

** It is estimated that 0.30 million tonnes of industrial wood waste is used for woodfuel and is thus already included in the woodfuel total. In addition, 0.08 million tonnes of wood waste is not used.

Table 4.2

LAND AREA BY REGION AND ECOLOGICAL ZONE (1000 HA.)

	Central Nairobi	Coast	Eastern	North-Eastern	Nyanza	Rift Valley	Western	Total
High Potential	1360	506	1953	-	1249	2626	823	8516
Medium Potential	27	915	1011	-	3	832	-	2789
Semi-Arid	-	6883	12612	12690	-	13425	-	45610
Total	1387	8304	15576	12690	1252	16883	823	56914

Before proceeding to describe in greater detail the rather
large number of land uses and their areas, it is useful at this
point to highlight the prevailing conditions of land-use in high
and medium potential lands. Of the twenty per cent of total land
area, or 11,305 thousand hectares, in these ecological zones,
about 25 per cent is presently cropped, about 40 per cent is
uncropped agricultural land (a large portion of which is
associated with grazing requirements), and about 12 per cent is
in natural forests or plantations, excluding forest within the
National Parks (61,000 ha). Table 4.3 provides these percentages
on a provincial basis.

Other land-uses which are not included in this table include
urban and rural settlement land, parks and reserves, and
rangeland. Large areas of rangeland exist in medium potential
land in Coast and Eastern provinces. The significance of the
above figures is twofold: first, they show the lands associated
with the existing agricultural and wood resource bases; and
second, they indicate the scope and constraints in attempting to
expand these bases. Since large increases in domestic food
production are necessary to meet the needs of the expanding
population and since the Development Plan and National Food
Policy target no conversions of land under export crops and no
further destruction of forest land, the limited productive land
resources in Kenya must be allocated and utilized efficiently if
food and fuelwood requirements are to be satisfied in the future.
The agricultural and wood resource policies necessary to meet
this challenge will be discussed in subsequent sections of this
volume.

A full list of the existing land-use types in Kenya that
have been specified in this study is given in Table 4.4, where
land areas are given on a provincial and national basis,
aggregated over ecological zones.

The detailed regional and ecological zone breakdown is given
in Volume 1 of the support material, along with the sources and
methods of estimations. Here, it is useful to clarify this table
by drawing attention to three points.

The first point concerns the distinction between
agricultural land use categories. Large and small farms are
broken down by the average size of holding. Twenty hectares was
taken as the dividing point in accordance with published sources.
Food crops include all land planted to food, including sugarcane.
Temporary crops refer to temporary industrial crops, such as
pyrethrum and cotton. Permanent crops are cash crops,
predominantly coffee, tea, and cashew nuts. Uncropped land is
uncultivated land used for grazing and social activities.

The second point concerns the distinction between rangeland,
savannah bush, and savannah grass. While all three categories
can, in fact, be considered rangeland, this particular name is
used to refer to uncultivated medium potential land that could be
cultivated in the future. Savannah bush refers to semi-arid land

Table 4.3

DISTRIBUTION OF HIGH AND MEDIUM POTENTIAL LAND BY MAJOR LAND-USES (PERCENT)

	Central Nairobi	Coast	Eastern	North-Eastern	Nyanza	Rift Valley	Western	Total
Cropped	42	18	27	-	38	13	45	26
Uncropped and Grazing	28	12	39	-	55	61	43	43
Forest	17	8	5	-	0	17	8	10
Other	13	62	29	-	7	9	4	21
Total	100	100	100	-	100	100	100	100

LAND USE BY PROVINCE (1000 HA.)

Land Use, Category	Central Nairobi	Coast	Eastern	North-Eastern	Nyanza	Rift Valley	Western	Total
Large Farm Food	15	7	10		15	160	6	213
Large Farm Temp. Crops	25		6		1	115		147
Large Farm Perm. Crops	38	33	13		1	48		133
Large Farm Uncropped	256	45	246		12	1698	3	2260
Small Farm Food	404	113	690		424	133	323	2086
Small Farm Temporary	11	3	13		23	4	31	85
Small Farm Permanent	93	97	70		17	4	4	284
Small Farm Uncropped	128	132	902		664	403	353	2582
Urban Built Env.	13	6	4	2	4	8	2	39
Rural Built Env.	37	45	112		50	92	31	366
Parks/Reserves*	121	1633	1245	53	35	562	1	3650
Natural Forests (Excluding Nat. Parks)	205	118	132		3	653	56	1166
Woodlot	4		1			15	1	21
Plantation	25	2	9		1	87	11	135
Savannah Bush		3049	3430	6796		6795		20070
Savannah Grass		2398	8061	5839		5999		22296
Rangeland	12	622	634		3	107		1379
Total	1387	8304	15576	12690	1252	16883	823	56914
* Forests within National Parks	42	-	0	-	-	19	-	61

with a canopy cover of greater than two per cent, while savannah grass signifies semi-arid land of less than two per cent canopy cover. While these are not land use categories per se, they were devised to be consistent with the aims of the study.

Third, natural forests include both the areas associated with non-commercial species (including bamboo) which are used primarily for rural fuelwood and construction poles, and commercial species which are used for wood feedstocks in construction, pulp, and paper industries. Plantations are divided into woodlots containing eucalyptus and wattle, which mainly meet woodfuel construction needs. Other forest plantations, including cypress and pine forests, are associated with construction and industrial feedstock demands. Wood resources for fuelwood requirements are found more generally outside the forests on agricultural and semi-arid lands.

Standing Stocks and Yields of Wood Resources

Estimations of standing stocks and yields of woody biomass for the various regional land types in Kenya were made on the basis of surveys and measurements undertaken by foresters working on the project as well as recorded statistics. (For further details, readers should consult the technical volumes). Three separate categories of the wood resource base were identified in these procedures, each of which was further broken down by region, ecozone, and land type. These three are: wood resources in forests (including various natural forest types and plantations), wood resources in low potential lands (primarily savannah and rangelands) comprising more than eighty percent of Kenya's land area, and wood resources on high and medium potential lands (primarily on the various agricultural land types).

Forest stocks and yields of woody biomass were estimated on the basis of detailed knowledge of the specific forest land areas, their ecological characteristics, and the characteristics and conditions of the various species within each forest area identified. These include the average size and ages of trees, their typical growth pattern, and the conditions of management where applicable. In addition, in order to estimate woody biomass by weight, typical volume to weight ratios were applied, ranging from 1.98 cubic meters per tonne for cypress and pine to 1.06 cubic meters per tonne for mangrove. All ratios were calculated assuming 15 per cent moisture content.

While no separate land area within natural forests exists for commercial species, the wood stocks and yields from this portion of natural forests were added separately since they often differ and are principally allocated to industrial and construction feedstock uses. Moreover, due to the protected status of natural forest there may be greater incentive and opportunity to apply management techniques here (e.g. thinning) with the objective of increasing stocks and yields. It should be noted that, in general, despite the primary use of these wood resources, substantial residues (more than fifty per cent of total wood offtake left as branches and tops in the forest and cuttings and scrap at the mills) are available for fuelwood. An estimated 0.27 million tonnes out of 0.77 million tonnes of industrial wood is used as fuel, but more is available for use. Also, some of the industrial wood products are burnt when their useful life is over.

Non-industrial species (including scrub and bamboo) are available for fuelwood and construction wood under conditions when other wood resources more directly accessible to the population are exhausted. Plantations have been divided into two groups: those such as cypress, pine, and other species (including some hardwoods) that are used as industrial and construction feedstock; and those (such as eucalyptus and wattle) which serve primarily local fuel and construction requirements. The stocks and yields on existing plantations reflect conditions of various stages of maturity. Thus, it is expected that these will increase over the next twenty years.

Woody biomass resource estimates for high and medium potential lands were made on the basis of mensuration surveys undertaken in Kenya in 1981 as part of the project. Similarly, the wood resource base in rangelands was estimated on the basis of detailed survey and analysis. These surveys are described in Volumes 1 and 2 of the technical analysis. Tables 4.5 and 4.6 summarize the results of the wood resource estimations made during the course of the project. These results are presented on a per-hectare basis in order to highlight the different overall ecological and land-use conditions on a provincial basis in Kenya. Tables 4.7 and 4.8, which follow, provide wood resource information in terms of estimated physical stocks and yields.

Beyond the immediate wood production characteristics of the various land areas in Kenya, other factors influence the relationship between the availability of wood resources and the demand for these resources. These include the geographic and socio-economic conditions affecting access to and movements of wood and wood derived commodities. In particular, although each land area produces given quantities of wood, not all of this can serve to meet wood requirements. For each land type a parameter which measures accessibility to wood resources has been estimated. The accessibility fraction is a measure of a more specific relationship which includes: distance of population to wood resources, limits to household labour time budget allocated to fuelwood gathering, availability of tools and labour, and privatization of land. We shall return to this concept below.

As discussed earlier, each of the major categories of wood demand is associated in a particular way with the various wood resource bases. Fuelwood and rural construction demands are met

Table 4.5

WOOD STOCKS BY PROVINCE, ECOZONE, AND LAND TYPE* (TONNES/HA)

Ecozone	Land Use	Central/Nairobi	Coast	Eastern	North-Eastern	Nyanza	Rift Valley	Western
High	Large Farm	15.80	28.80	13.10	–	18.00	10.60	10.20
	Small Farm	15.80	12.50	13.10	–	7.80	9.80	7.90
	Rural Built	3.68	1.68	3.71	–	2.90	1.38	2.69
	Urban Built	4.80	2.50	6.80	–	3.20	5.80	8.00
	Parks/Reserves	69.40	37.20	45.00	–	41.40	66.90	54.70
	Natural Forest	94.40	49.30	67.20	–	63.00	119.60	118.23
	Woodlot	285.10	329.60	264.90	–	69.00	154.80	61.40
	Plantation	194.10	152.40	185.70	–	125.00	158.00	102.10
Medium	Large Farm	–	–	–	–	–	8.20	–
	Small Farm	–	4.60	4.60	–	–	7.90	–
	Rural Built	–	1.01	1.01	–	–	0.98	–
	Urban Built	4.80	2.50	6.80	–	–	5.80	–
	Parks/Reserves	26.42	22.85	37.00	–	–	21.56	–
	Natural Forest	–	–	56.25	–	–	95.70	–
	Plantation	–	–	–	–	–	–	–
	Rangeland	26.42	22.85	37.00	–	21.55	21.56	–
Semi-Arid	Urban Built	–	–	–	15.04	–	–	–
	Parks/Reserves	–	12.81	13.62	–	–	13.89	–
	Natural Forest	–	–	–	–	–	95.70	–
	Savannah Bush	–	22.85	37.00	24.34	–	21.56	–
	Savannah Grass	–	5.54	3.70	4.20	–	5.00	–

* Variation between provinces reflects variation in the age and distribution of trees.

Table 4.6

WOOD YIELDS BY PROVINCE, ECOZONE, AND LAND TYPE.* (TONNES/HA/ANNUM)

Ecozone	Land Use	Central/ Nairobi	Coast	Eastern	North- Eastern	Nyanza	Rift Valley	Western
High	Large Farm	1.05	1.92	0.87	–	1.20	0.71	0.68
	Small Farm	1.05	0.83	0.87	–	0.52	0.65	0.53
	Rural Built	0.24	0.11	0.25	–	0.19	0.09	0.18
	Urban Built	0.30	0.20	0.40	–	0.20	0.40	0.60
	Parks/Reserves	2.40	1.30	2.30	–	1.40	2.10	2.10
	Natural Forest	2.98	1.36	2.83	–	1.71	3.11	3.57
	Woodlot	28.51	32.84	17.66	–	6.90	16.06	3.07
	Plantation	6.47	5.08	2.68	–	4.18	5.27	2.92
Medium	Large Farm	–	–	–	–	–	0.55	–
	Small Farm	–	0.31	0.31	–	–	0.53	–
	Rural Built	–	0.07	0.07	–	–	0.06	–
	Urban Built	0.30	0.20	0.40	–	–	0.40	–
	Parks/Reserves	0.65	0.54	0.96	–	–	0.50	–
	Natural Forest	–	–	2.14	–	–	2.73	–
	Plantation	–	–	–	–	–	–	–
	Rangeland	0.65	0.54	0.96	–	0.50	0.50	–
Semi-Arid	Urban Built	–	–	–	0.35	–	–	–
	Parks/Reserves	–	0.34	0.33	–	–	0.32	–
	Natural Forest	–	–	–	0.59	–	2.73	–
	Savannah Bush	–	0.54	0.96	0.08	–	0.50	–
	Savannah Grass	–	0.10	0.07	–	–	0.09	–

* Variation between provinces reflects variation in the age and distribution of trees.

Table 4.7

TOTAL WOOD STOCKS BY PROVINCE AND LAND TYPE (MILLION TONNES)

Land Use Category	Central/ Nairobi	Coast	Eastern	North- Eastern	Nyanza	Rift Valley	Western	Total
Large Farm Food	0.24	0.20	0.12	-	0.27	1.61	0.06	2.5
Large Farm Temp.	0.39	0.01	0.08	-	0.01	1.15	-	1.6
Large Farm Perm.	0.60	0.96	0.17	-	0.02	0.51	-	2.2
Large Farm Uncrpd.	4.05	1.29	3.22	-	0.21	17.02	0.03	25.8
Small Farm Food	6.38	0.90	7.15	-	3.31	1.27	2.55	21.5
Small Farm Temp.	0.17	0.03	0.09	-	0.18	0.04	0.25	0.7
Small Farm Perm.	1.46	1.21	0.92	-	0.13	0.04	0.03	3.7
Small Farm Uncrpd.	2.02	1.65	11.82	-	5.18	3.95	2.79	27.4
Urban Built Env.	0.06	0.02	0.03	-	0.01	0.04	0.02	0.1
Rural Built Env.	0.14	0.05	0.31	-	0.14	0.12	0.08	0.8
Parks/Reserves	7.91	29.92	20.10	0.80	1.44	12.64	0.05	65.8
Natural Forests	19.31	5.84	8.66	-	0.21	69.28	6.62	109.9
Woodlot	1.19	0.08	0.27	-	-	2.30	0.03	3.8
Plantation	4.92	0.34	1.62	-	0.09	13.79	1.15	21.9
Savannah Bush	-	69.68	126.90	165.41	-	146.50	-	508.4
Savannah Grass	-	13.28	29.82	24.52	-	29.99	-	97.6
Rangeland	0.33	14.22	23.45	-	0.06	2.31	-	40.3
Total	49.17	139.68	234.73	190.73	11.26	302.56	13.66	934.8

Table 4.8
TOTAL WOOD YIELDS BY PROVINCE AND LAND TYPE (1000 TONNES/ANNUM)

Land Use Category	Central/ Nairobi	Coast	Eastern	North- Eastern	Nyanza	Rift Valley	Western	Total
Large Farm Food	40	10	10	-	100	110	20	290
Large Farm Temp.	60	-	-	-	-	80	-	140
Large Farm Perm.	90	60	10	-	10	30	-	200
Large Farm Uncrpd.	610	70	200	-	70	1160	10	2120
Small Farm Food	480	40	130	-	1010	40	740	2440
Small Farm Temp.	10	-	-	-	30	-	70	110
Small Farm Perm.	110	60	10	-	20	-	10	210
Small Farm Uncrpd.	150	80	180	-	1130	130	800	2470
Urban Built Env.	-	-	-	-	-	-	-	-
Rural Built Env.	20	-	20	-	50	10	30	130
Parks/Reserves	120	70	70	-	60	60	-	380
Natural Forests	600	30	70	-	10	320	590	1620
Woodlot	120	10	20	-	-	240	-	390
Plantation	160	10	20	-	-	460	30	680
Savannah Bush	-	1010	2250	480	-	3040	-	6780
Savannah Grass	-	160	420	60	-	550	-	1190
Rangeland	40	330	660	-	20	80	-	1130
Total	2630	1940	4070	540	2510	6310	2300	20280

by local wood resources primarily on agricultural lands, existing
woodlots, residues from construction and feedstock wood gathering
and processing activities, and as necessary from non-commercial
species in natural forests from within regions. Charcoal demands,
on the other hand, from each region are met by wood resources
(after conversion to charcoal) from neighboring regions as well
as the region itself. As a measure of this, a matrix of
inter-regional charcoal movements has been developed to account
for such geographic supply/demand relationships. Finally,
industrial and construction feedstock requirements are met on a
national basis by wood resources available primarily from managed
forest plantations, as well as from commercial species in natural
forests. These relationships are geographic and economic since
the commodity character of charcoal and the products deriving
from wood feedstocks make it more cost-beneficial to transport
these items. In addition, there are diseconomies in transporting
fuelwood over long distances under current conditions. However,
several industries such as tobacco curing and tea drying have
overcome this obstacle by growing the fuelwood near the factory.
Also, the economic transport distance could be increased by
pre-drying, densifying and pelletization. Detailed cost estimates
are contained in the technical volume on economic policy and wood
resources.

Land Productivity in Agriculture

As we have stressed, the energy problem cannot be adequately
addressed without consideration of the developmental context
within Kenya. One of the more pressing goals expressed in the
most recent Five Year Plan is the attainment of self-sufficiency
in food production. The fact that the arable land resources of
the country are so limited implies that food production
requirements be taken as a constraint within which the energy
needs of the population must be met. In order to do this, it is
necessary first to get a picture of the current food requirements
and production possibilities. These requirements can then be
projected into the future to see how land use patterns and
therefore potential woodfuel supplies will change to account for
the increased demand for food. Because the focus of this
modelling effort is on energy, rough estimates of food
requirements and agricultural production are sufficient to give a
relative picture of required land use adjustments.

After examination of the estimates for food production and
consumption that exist for Kenya, it was decided that the
estimates from the National Food Policy Paper (17) are the most
consistent and pose the fewest discrepancies. Table 1 of that
paper gives estimates of production of the nine major food
products consumed in Kenya in 1980. Of these nine products, only
seven were directly ascribed to the land use accounting system

used in the analysis, i.e. agricultural crops. Meat and dairy products are asssumed to be produced primarily in uncropped agricultural lands and rangelands. Some adjustments were also made to include agricultural crops not included in the list from the Food Policy Paper. The estimates of base-year food production and requirements are provided in Table 4.9.

In order to capture the future agriculture output properly, as land is brought into production in different regions and farm types (e.g. smallholder and largeholder), estimates were developed of agriculture productivity on an output per hectare basis. A summary is presented in Table 4.10 below. The differences can be ascribed to a combination of different crop mixes as well as the variation in average land productivity.

Current Wood Use Patterns

As has already been indicated, the total demand for wood has three components: for fuelwood, for wood to produce charcoal, and for wood as industrial feedstock. In the base year, 1980, total demand for wood has been estimated at 20.82 million metric tonnes, of which 12.83 million tonnes (61 per cent) was for fuelwood, 6.81 million tonnes (33 per cent) for use in the production of charcoal, 0.4 million tonnes (2 per cent) for use as rural housebuilding and fencing poles, and 0.8 million tonnes for industrial feedstock and construction timber. However, an estimated 0.3 million tonnes of this wood is used as fuelwood and has already been counted. This wood is supplied from resources that are found on the various land types in Kenya. Fuelwood is drawn largely from the standing timber on agricultural land; charcoal is drawn mainly from agricultural, range and bushland; and industrial feedstock is supplied predominantly from managed plantations and commercial species in the natural forests. This section discusses the current supply of and demand for wood resources for industrial, fuelwood, and charcoal purposes. Table 4.11 contains details of the national wood demand.

Rural Construction Wood

Rural construction uses wood resources that generally do not come from large managed plantations. The sources of supply for rural construction often coincide with fuelwood supply sources. The requirements for wood in rural areas, for poles used in fencing and other construction purposes, comprised a significant portion of total national wood resource demand. It is instructive to break out this demand separately for a number of reasons, rather than, say, aggregating it with industrial construction-wood feedstock demand. First, this demand will depend primarily on rural population and its expansion over time.

Table 4.9

ESTIMATED FOOD PRODUCTION FOR BASE YEAR 1980

Crops	Estimated Production (1000 Tonnes)
Maize	1942+
Wheat Flour	142
Sorghum/Millet	369
Rice	23
Beans	140
Potatoes	450
Sugar	402*
Other	971

+ According to the Sessional Paper, 1980 was an anomalously low year for maize production. Following the suggestion made there, the average of the 1976 and 1980 figure has been used here.

* Sugar is included as net refined sugar; the cane total is about 4 million tonnes.

Table 4.10

AGRICULTURAL PRODUCTIVITY (TONNES/HA)

Category	Central	Coast	Eastern	North-Eastern	Nyanza	Rift Valley	Western
Food	3.52	3.99	1.37	-	3.05	2.74	2.69
Temporary Crops	0.22	1.26	0.55	-	0.57	0.44	0.38
Permanent Crops	2.99	1.09	0.60	-	1.26	1.25	2.52

Table 4.11

PROVINCIAL AND NATIONAL WOOD SUPPLY AND DEMAND - BASE CASE* (MILLION TONNES)

Source of Demand	Central/Nairobi	Coast	Eastern	North-Eastern	Nyanza	Rift Valley	Western	Total
Local Woodfuel Demand	2.46	1.94	3.11	.48	2.51	3.94	1.98	–
Woodfuel Demand Other Regions	–	–	.94	.06	–	1.91	.30	–
Subtotal Woodfuel Demand	2.46	1.94	4.06	.54	2.51	5.85	2.28	19.64
Feedstock Demand	.18	.01	.03	–	–	.51	.04	.77
Total Demand	2.64	1.95	4.09	.54	2.51	6.36	2.32	20.41
Source of Supply								
Sustainable Supply	.99	1.62	3.06	.54	.38	4.17	.31	11.07
Supply from Stocks	1.63	.33	1.02	–	2.13	2.14	2.00	9.26
Total Supply	2.62	1.95	4.08	.54	2.51	6.31	2.31	20.33
Shortfall	.02	–	–	–	–	.05	–	.08

Woodfuel demand from other regions stands for wood demand for charcoal from other regions, i.e. exports of charcoal to other regions.

* Rural Pole demand is omitted from this table.

Moreover, it is a local demand serviced in the main by local wood resources. Finally, the resources provided to meet this demand are generally obtained from trees outside the large forest plantations and commercial species in natural forests, both of which service primarily modern sector construction and feedstock demands. The rural construction wood requirements are met primarily from non-commercial species in natural forests (including bamboo), from trees outside the forests, and from small woodlot plantations in rural areas. Thus, the burden that this demand places on wood resources is distributed differently than industrial/construction wood feedstock demand. As such, we have integrated the rural construction demand with the demand for woodfuel.

The estimates of the current demand for rural construction poles in Kenya is about 420,000 tonnes of wood (6.7 PJ). This demand alone is about the same magnitude as the final demand of all the industrial/construction wood feedstock demands combined, and accounts for about 2 per cent of total national demand for wood resources in Kenya.

Feedstocks

Industrial wood and feedstock includes all milled lumber that is processed for use as paper and pulp, panelling, and urban construction. The final demand for wood in this sector is about 0.4 million tonnes (6.5 PJ). However, about 0.8 million tonnes of roundwood are required to produce the final product. This is illustrated in Table 4.12.

Substantial quantities of waste in the form of branches, tops, bark, offcuts and sawdust etc. are potentially available for use and it is estimated that bout 0.32 million tonnes out of 0.369 million tonnes are in fact used, thus the effective demand for industrial roundwood is of the order of 0.4 million tonnes.

Eighty-five per cent of the base-year demand for feedstock is met from the sustainable yield of the managed plantation areas in Kenya. The remaining fifteen per cent is taken from existing commercial species found in the natural forest areas.

The base-year demand for fuelwood, 12.83 million tonnes, represents largely the demand for rural energy consumption in both tne domestic and industrial sectors. As mentioned earlier, this wood is drawn from the standing timber remaining on agricultural land, uncropped land, and rangeland according to the proportion of that timber deemed to be accessible. Unlike feedstock demand, fuelwood demand must be satisfied from local sources. A rule-of-thumb in the East African context is that wood can be economically transported only for distances less than eighty kilometers by road. For this reason, it is assumed in the analysis that the regional demand for fuelwood is met primarily by supplies within the provinces. People generally do not travel

Table 4.12

DEMAND FOR INDUSTRIAL/CONSTRUCTION WOOD FEEDSTOCK (1980)
UNITS 1000 TONNES

Product	Roundwood Requirements	Wood in Finished Product	Waste
Industrial Poles	60	50	10
Pitsawn Timber	140	55	85
Machinesawn Timber	275	125	150
Panel Products	40	26	14
Pulp (and paper)	255	153	102
Total	770	409	361

large distances to collect firewood. The little wood that is transported commercially is generally subject to the 80 Km limit. While cases where fuelwood is transported significant distances can be found, they are few.

The second factor limiting the availability of wood for fuelwood is accessibility, a complex factor for taking into consideration the effect of technology, tree succession, land privatization, and distance on the rural population's potential fuelwood supply. The first component of accessibility, the technological factor, is taken to represent the proportion of trees on a given land type that can be cut by those harvesting the fuelwood, (e.g., by using a panga for smallholders) plus an additional proportion to account for branchwood and deadwood. The technical factor is then multiplied by a factor representing the locational accessibility for a given land use type. Accessibility is, therefore, a combination of the ability to harvest wood and the location of population centers relative to those wood supplies. Its calculation includes no consideration for privatization as the measure was designed to be a maximum accessibility assuming that, under conditions of scarcity, households would obtain access to whatever woodstocks were available, either directly or through commoditization. On smallholder land the accessibility proportion ranges from 0.2 for Eastern province to 0.6 for Western province. For largeholders, the proportion is 0.8 as they are assumed to have greater technical accessibility. The accessibility measure does not take into account the possibility that technological means for harvesting fuelwood may change as supplies become increasingly scarce. Future research needs to focus more closely on the determinants of accessibility and its impacts on fuel availability.

The demand for charcoal (6.81 million tonnes of wood) represents a demand for domestic energy that is predominantly urban in nature. Urban households depend heavily upon charcoal as a source of energy for cooking primarily because of the non-transportability of wood: charcoal can bear transportation whereas wood cannot. Wood for charcoal comes primarily from agricultural land, rangeland, and bushland, but it is not limited to local sources as is the demand for fuelwood. It is free to flow between regions according to the proportions established by a charcoal transport matrix developed on the basis of estimated inter-regional exchanges. The national demand for charcoal is broken down provincially by the proportion of total urban population which is located within each province. In this way, it is represented as a predominantly urban phenomenon.

The charcoal matrix is designed to represent the proportion of charcoal consumed within one province supplied from outside provinces. As such, it controls the flows of charcoal within and between regions. For every province, the matrix represents the proportion of charcoal which is supplied from that province itself, and the proportion which is supplied from every other province. The proportions are based on field observation. For Central/Nairobi province, ten per cent of the charcoal comes from within the province, thirty percent comes from Eastern, and sixty percent from Rift Valley. These estimates were based on interviews with charcoal dealers in Nairobi and adjusted to account for other cities in the province.

The national supply of and demand for wood is broken down by province and type of wood-demand in Table 4.1. The top portion of the table gives total woodfuel demand from within the province and woodfuel exports (in the form of charcoal) from that province to other provinces. These sum together with the estimates of feedstock demand within the region to produce total wood demand for the province. The bottom half of the table provides estimates of how these demands are met. The first figure gives that portion of regional wood demand that is met through the harvesting of sustainable yield from existing woodstocks. The second figure is an estimate of the quantity of wood demand that is met through the cutting of standing stocks. These two figures sum to equal the provincial and national demand estimates. Note that there is no shortfall in wood supply for the base year. While there may be pockets of unmet demand in the base year, as witnessed to by the percent of total rural energy that is attributable to dung and crop wastes (4 per cent of total rural biomass consumption), supply and demand are assumed to be in balance.

Two patterns emerging from the table warrant discussion at this point. The first is that the demand for wood from other regions is significant in only four provinces: Eastern, Rift Valley, Western and Northeastern. This is the case because extra charcoal supply is required for the cities in surrounding regions. Eastern and Rift Valley are charcoal exporters to Nairobi; Western and Rift Valley supply charcoal to Kisimu; and Northeastern supplies a small amount of charcoal to Mombasa. These patterns are as would be expected from given transportation routes and the interregional flow of charcoal.

The second point to emerge is that the high population density provinces, Central, Nyanza, and Western, have already begun the process of cutting woodstocks. In each of the provinces, over half of the wood is supplied from existing stocks instead of sustainable yield. There is currently insufficient wood available on a sustained yield basis to meet all of the wood demand in the regions. Woodstocks are being cut at a rate which can only exacerbate the future wood shortage and lead to further environmental degredation. The cutting of wood stocks signifies the beginning of a process which leads to a more serious set of social and environmental problems.

CHAPTER 5. BASE CASE PROJECTIONS

     In the previous chapters, the current (1980) pattern of Kenyan energy supply and demand has been described. The function of that exercise was twofold: first, to illuminate the present energy situation with respect to the quantitative linkages between primary sources, conversions and end-use demands; and, second, to provide a detailed departure point (the "base year") for long-range projections of Kenya's energy future (demands, requirements, land-use patterns, regional wood shortages, etc.). This section describes those projections.

     Reliable forecasts of future energy supply/demand pictures require two components. First, a mathematical model is required which is capable of accurately simulating the real-world structure determining energy demand and resources. For this investigation, a computer-based system has been created which is designed for disaggregated projections of end-use demand resources, regional biomass availability, land-use constraints, and so on. This planning tool, the LDC Energy Alternatives Planning (LEAP) system is described in technical volume 9.

     The second requirement of a reliable forecast is that it incorporate a self-consistent and realistic set of assumptions on the evolution of the primary driving variables which effect the level and character of energy requirements. Broadly categorized, there are five major classes of variables effecting the evolution of energy demand/supply patterns:

economic   (income, trade, prices, etc.)

demographic   (population, household formation, urbanization, etc.)

technological   (equipment, processes, agricultural practices, etc.)

institutional   (values, customs, tenurial patterns, etc.)

policy   (regulation, subsidy, pricing, promotion, etc.)

These five dimensions, of course, are not independent, rather they are mutually and interactively conditioning. A projection requires, then, not only a capable mathematical simulation tool, but analytically interesting assumptions on this cluster of variables.

     The function of the Base Case is to provide a bench-mark for guiding in the development of energy policy initiatives. It should establish the timeframe, type, and magnitude of problems emerging in energy sufficiency under "business-as-usual" conditions. Therefore, the Base Case attempts to incorporate best estimates of the regular unfolding of socio-economic variables, e.g. targeted economic growth, evolving demographic patterns, and, most importantly here, continuity in Kenyan energy policy.

As will become apparant in the following, the Base Case projection is not a realistic, or even possible outcome. Major inconsistencies between demand and possible supply will rapidly develop under the assumptions adopted. The development path outlined in the Base Case projection can therefore not really happen. It is merely developed here in order to illustrate the approximate timing and scale of the problems that arise ahead. Consistency between demand and supply requires major policy initiatives, some of which will have to be initiated within the near future if severe social disruption is going to be avoided. The Base Case projections, as developed in this Chapter, will provide the basis for development of a prescriptive Policy Case projection with the inclusion of energy programme targets which deviate from business-as-usual assumptions. Specifically, the Base Case assumption of energy policy continuity will be relaxed and it will be suggested that unprecedented levels of policy effort are required to avoid serious problems in the future. But first, the Base Case projections - and the energy problems it foretells - are described below.

Demand

Base Case energy demand projections have been performed, using the LEAP system, to the end of the century. The key demographic and economic assumptions employed are discussed later in this chapter. Here we summarize the major forecast findings.

The growth in end-use demand is shown in Figure 5.1. Total demand is projected to grow at an average annual growth rate of 4.6 per cent. Wood and charcoal end-use consumption grow at 3.8 per cent and 5.9 per cent per annum, respectively, reflecting an increasing trend toward urbanization. Oil consumption grows at 6.1 per cent per annum, from 15.4 million barrels annually in 1980 to 41.5 million barrels in 2000. Sectoral projections of demand disaggregated by fuel type are displayed in Table 5.1. Because provision has to be made for total wood supply, not just woodfuel projections have been made for rural poles and industrial wood, and these are also given in the table in terms of energy equivalents. Likewise, jet fuel to supply international planes, while not domestic consumption, has still to be planned for.

Demographic Considerations

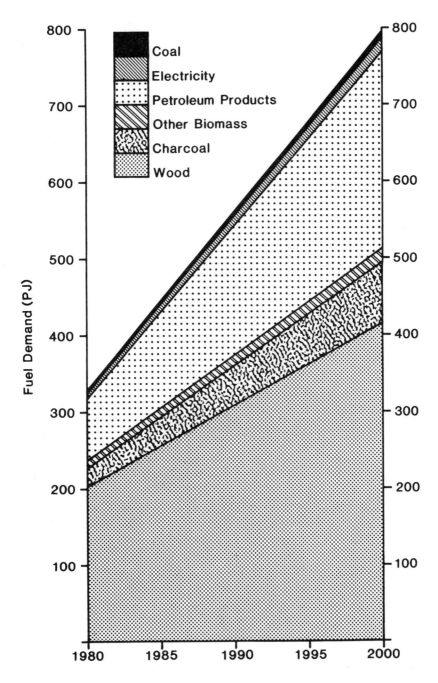

Figure 5.1 Base – Case Forecast of
End – Use Fuel Consumption

Table 5.1

BASE CASE SECTORAL PROJECTIONS (PJ)

Level/Year	1980	1985	1990	1995	2000
SECTOR					
Urban Household	21.45	35.35	49.14	71.93	94.84
Fuelwood	3.03	5.27	7.74	11.67	15.83
Charcoal	12.66	20.83	28.92	42.44	56.10
Bottled Gas	0.79	1.23	1.62	2.27	2.85
Kerosene	2.90	4.81	6.73	9.93	13.20
Electricity	2.08	3.20	4.14	5.63	6.85
SECTOR					
Rural Household	172.98	207.98	242.63	285.40	328.15
Fuelwood	150.56	181.46	212.21	250.06	288.04
Charcoal	9.25	10.75	12.12	13.89	15.55
Biomass/Residue	2.81	3.43	4.06	4.83	5.62
Kerosene	4.19	4.99	5.77	6.73	7.69
Maize	6.17	7.34	8.48	9.88	11.26
SECTOR					
Agriculture	8.23	9.56	10.93	12.46	14.05
Diesel	6.63	7.57	8.51	9.46	10.40
Electricity	0.59	0.83	1.11	1.55	2.05
Petrol	1.02	1.16	1.31	1.45	1.60
SECTOR					
Informal Ind Urban	1.45	2.32	3.20	4.53	5.86
Fuelwood	0.39	0.63	0.86	1.22	1.58
Charcoal	0.95	1.53	2.10	2.97	3.85
Biomass/Residue	0.00	0.00	0.00	0.00	0.00
Bottled Gas	0.00	0.00	0.00	0.00	0.00
Kerosene	0.07	0.11	0.15	0.21	0.27
Diesel	0.01	0.01	0.02	0.02	0.03
Electricity	0.02	0.04	0.05	0.07	0.09
Petrol	0.01	0.02	0.02	0.03	0.04
SECTOR					
Informal Ind Rural	32.48	38.33	44.17	50.73	57.28
Fuelwood	30.41	35.88	41.35	47.49	53.63
Charcoal	2.07	2.44	2.82	3.23	3.65
SECTOR					
Large Industry	45.82	66.34	86.86	126.63	166.41
Fuelwood	17.44	24.03	30.61	42.18	53.74
Lumber	6.30	8.53	10.75	14.57	18.38
Bottled Gas	0.17	0.27	0.36	0.55	0.74
Kerosene	0.91	1.39	1.87	2.87	3.87
Residual Oil	17.92	27.29	36.65	56.06	76.47
Coal	1.31	2.07	2.83	4.47	6.11
Electricity	1.77	2.78	3.79	5.95	8.10
SECTOR					
Transportation	45.38	62.84	80.29	108.37	136.46
Diesel	13.56	18.35	23.14	31.15	39.15
Jet Fuel	11.89	16.28	20.68	28.60	36.52
Residual Oil	2.52	3.46	4.40	6.09	7.77
Electricity	0.05	0.05	0.05	0.05	0.05
Petrol	17.35	24.69	32.02	42.49	52.96
SECTOR					
Commercial	4.21	5.69	7.18	9.47	11.77
Fuelwood	1.60	1.99	2.38	2.89	3.39
Charcoal	0.39	0.48	0.58	0.70	0.82
Bottled Gas	0.25	0.36	0.47	0.66	0.86
Kerosene	0.10	0.15	0.19	0.27	0.36
Residual Oil	0.57	0.82	1.08	1.54	2.00
Solar	0.00	0.00	0.00	0.00	0.01
Electricity	1.31	1.89	2.48	3.41	4.33

The Kenyan population is growing more rapidly than any other national population in the world, at an annual rate of 3.9 per cent. The proximate explanation of this high rate of natural increase is simple: fertility levels are quite high, with a crude birth rate of 53 births per thousand of population, and mortality levels are low, with a crude death rate of 14 per thousand. A deeper explanation of the rapid rate of population growth lies in the historical pattern of economic development in Kenya, which has led to expansion of health and medical services but has not yet motivated significant declines in desired family size.

Estimation of the growth and spatial distribution of the Kenyan population over the next twenty years must be based upon a careful assessment of historical changes in Kenya over the last twenty years, as well as some consideration of the demographic history of countries at similar levels of economic development. Several important points emerge from the extended discussion of these topics in the technical volume on issues in energy policy.

A series of census results and exceptionally high quality surveys show that fertility levels have increased in Kenya over the last 15 years, from a total fertility rate (average births per surviving female) of 6.8 in 1962 to 8.1 in 1978. Some of this increase may be attributed to improvements in maternal health and concomitant increases in successful pregnancies, but certain social changes, such as the decline in polygamous marriages, have also had a positive effect on fertility. As many researchers have noted, the economic incentives for rearing children remain quite high, and the "Knowledge, Attitudes, Practices" Survey of 1977/78 showed very high levels of desired family size, at an average of eight children. Studies also show that expansion of family planning services has succeeded in improving awareness of contraceptive techniques, but has not contributed significantly to fertility decline.

Failure to recognize the persistence of high levels of desired family size has contributed to a tendency to overestimate potential for fertility decline in Kenya. While several projections made in the early 1970s were based on the assumption that the total fertility rate (TFR) might fall to 4 or even to 3 by the year 2000, more recent projections have explored the possibility that the TFR might remain at approximately 8 or even increase by the year 2000. The effect of improvements in maternal health on fertility, however, have probably been fully realized, and the two fertility scenarios that currently appear most plausible are:

(a) decline in the TFR to 6 in the year 2000, which is probably the most realistic decline that could be expected to accompany rapid economic development, and

(b) constant levels of average fertility, which may persist if economic development and urbanization are insufficient to reduce the economic incentives for large families.

Life expectancy in Kenya has risen from an estimated 40-45 years
in 1962 to 48.5 in 1969 to 53.5 in 1977. Many observers agree
that an overall life expectancy of 60 is likely by the year 2000,
although significant interprovincial differences in mortality
will probably persist. If the pace of economic development is
slowed, anticipated reductions in mortality may not occur,
leaving mortality levels essentially unchanged. Because important
health services are already in place, it is unlikely that
mortality will increase.

Patterns and likely trends of spatial distribution of the
Kenyan population are more difficult to discern, largely because
of inadequacies of existing data. While the censuses of 1962 and
1969 provide a measure of lifetime migration, it was not until
the 1979 census that any questions relevant to calculation of
annual migration rates were included. The 1979 result shows that
Nairobi experienced net immigration of 10.6 per cent in the year
preceding the census, and Coastal and Rift provinces also
experienced net gains. They also suggest that the country as a
whole experienced a net immigration of 50,000. The pattern of
relative provincial growth rates (not including Nairobi) reflects
a significant amount of rural-rural migration to Rift and Coastal
provinces, and this is expected to decline in the future, as
rural-urban migration becomes relatively more important.

Kenya remains at a fairly modest level of urbanization, with
15 per cent of the population living in towns of 2000 or more.
Urbanization proceeded at an annual rate of about 7.5 per cent
between 1969 and 1979, although changes in definitions of urban
boundaries render comparisons in historical growth rates between
provinces quite difficult. The Ministry of Planning and other
sources estimate that approximately 30 per cent of Kenya's
population will be urbanized by the year 2000. The percentage
distribution of the urban population between the provinces hinges
largely upon assumptions regarding Nairobi's growth rate over the
period. While Nairobi could increase at an annual rate of 7 - 9
per cent over the next 20 years, efforts to slow its relative
growth could succeed in reducing its rate of annual increase to 5
per cent. The urban priorities outlined in the Government of
Kenya's Fourth Development Plan suggest that this is not an
unlikely prospect.

Changes in the size of Kenyan households over the next 20
years are quite probable. In 1979 average household size was
approximately 5.7 members. The historic trend towards decreasing
household size (about 8 per cent since 1969) is expected to
continue. For purposes of the current analysis the following
household size assumptions are used: urban households decreasing
from 4.4 to 4.0 persons per household between 1979 and 2000 and
rural households decreasing from 6.0 to 5.5 over the same period.
This decrease in household size will lead to an increase in per
capita consumption of household energy if the efficiency of

end-use devices remains constant, for per capita consumption of
energy (and other consumer goods) generally declines with
increasing household size. This fact has been taken into account
when forecasting household energy, poles and sawnwood
consumption. Of course, it is difficult to accurately forecast
household size. The interpretation that is adopted here, and
documented in the supporting technical volumes, assumes a
continuation of current demographic trends. This is not
necessarily going to happen especially if the labour shortage,
including a shortage of labour for fuelwood collection, forces
rural people to have larger families.

The probable future trends described above form a basis for
a series of projections of the Kenyan population to the year 2000
namely,

Case A: Constant Fertility, Constant Mortality.

Case B: Decline in TFR from 8 to 6, Constant
         Mortality.

Case C: Decline in TFR from 8 to 6, increase in life
         expectancy to 60 years.

Case D: Constant Fertility, increase in life
         expectancy to 60 years.

All of these cases make uniform assumptions regarding spatial
distribution of the population, and utilize 1979 Provincial level
Census data as a starting point for a cohort - components method
projection developed as part of the LEAP system. Details on
demographic assumptions are described in the volume on issues in
energy policy.

An optimistic view of Kenya's economic development path over
the next 20 years suggests that Case C is the most likely and it
is the one used as part of our Base Case projections. The Base
Case projections indicate that Kenya's population will grow at
the rapid rate of 3.86 per cent annually, with the lowest growth
occurring in Northeast province (2.36 per cent) and the highest
in Rift province (5.11 per cent). Because of the decline in
household size, households will grow at the significantly more
rapid rate of 4.56 per cent annually. By the year 2000, the total
population of Kenya will be 33,962,000 and 47 per cent of this
population will be under the age of 15. Base Case projections for
population and households are presented, respectively, in Tables
5.2 and 5.3 below.

Table 5.2
BASE CASE POPULATION PROJECTIONS

SUMMARY POPULATION PROJECTIONS (THOUSANDS)
KENYA - DECLINING MORTALITY, DECLINING FERTILITY - CASE C

Year	Nairobi	Nyanza	N-East	East	Central	Coast	West	Rift	Total
1979									
URBAN	828.	208.	60.	233.	129.	407.	106.	338.	2309.
RURAL	0.	2436.	314.	2479.	2217.	936.	1727.	2902.	13011.
Total	828.	2644.	374.	2712.	2346.	1343.	1833.	3240.	15319.
1980									
URBAN	882.	245.	65.	250.	139.	446.	121.	385.	2533.
RURAL	0.	2493.	319.	2559.	2293.	968.	1772.	3048.	13452.
Total	882.	2738.	384.	2809.	2432.	1415.	1893.	3432.	15985.
1985									
URBAN	1190.	459.	93.	347.	201.	683.	210.	686.	3870.
RURAL	0.	2749.	343.	2976.	2716.	1127.	1993.	3867.	15771.
Total	1190.	3208.	436.	3323.	2916.	1811.	2202.	4553.	19640.
1990									
URBAN	1549.	728.	127.	468.	282.	991.	321.	1122.	5589.
RURAL	0.	2968.	365.	3436.	3233.	1266.	2218.	4805.	18291.
Total	1549.	3696.	492.	3904.	3516.	2257.	2539.	5927.	23879.
1995									
URBAN	1935.	1058.	167.	618.	390.	1371.	459.	1712.	7709.
RURAL	0.	3161.	383.	3950.	3859.	1365.	2454.	5796.	20968.
Total	1935.	4219.	550.	4568.	4249.	2736.	2914.	7508.	28678.
2000									
URBAN	2330.	1459.	212.	801.	529.	1821.	630.	2462.	10243.
RURAL	0.	3330.	398.	4517.	4584.	1414.	2704.	6772.	23720.
Total	2330.	4789.	610.	5318.	5113.	3236.	3333.	9233.	33962.

Average Annual Growth Rates 1979-2000

URBAN	5.05%	9.72%	6.18%	6.05%	6.95%	7.40%	8.87%	9.91%	7.35%
RURAL	0.0%	1.50%	1.14%	2.90%	3.52%	1.99%	2.16%	4.12%	2.90%
Total	5.05%	2.87%	2.36%	3.26%	3.78%	4.28%	2.89%	5.11%	3.86%

Table 5.3
BASE CASE HOUSEHOLD PROJECTIONS

SUMMARY HOUSEHOLD PROJECTIONS (THOUSANDS)
KENYA - DECLINING MORTALITY, DECLINING FERTILITY - CASE C

Year	Nairobi	Nyanza	N-East	East	Central	Coast	West	Rift	Total
1979									
URBAN	188.	47.	14.	53.	29.	92.	24.	77.	525.
RURAL	0.	406.	52.	413.	369.	156.	288.	484.	2168.
Total	188.	453.	66.	466.	399.	248.	312.	561.	2693.
1980									
URBAN	201.	56.	15.	57.	32.	102.	28.	88.	578.
RURAL	0.	417.	53.	428.	384.	162.	296.	510.	2251.
Total	201.	473.	68.	485.	415.	264.	324.	598.	2829.
1985									
URBAN	278.	107.	22.	81.	47.	159.	49.	160.	903.
RURAL	0.	469.	59.	508.	464.	192.	340.	660.	2693.
Total	278.	576.	80.	589.	510.	352.	389.	820.	3595.
1990									
URBAN	370.	174.	30.	112.	67.	236.	77.	268.	1334.
RURAL	0.	517.	64.	599.	563.	221.	387.	837.	3188.
Total	370.	691.	94.	711.	631.	457.	463.	1105.	4521.
1995									
URBAN	472.	258.	41.	151.	95.	335.	112.	418.	1883.
RURAL	0.	562.	68.	703.	687.	243.	437.	1032.	3732.
Total	472.	821.	109.	854.	782.	578.	549.	1449.	5614.
2000									
URBAN	582.	365.	53.	200.	132.	455.	157.	615.	2561.
RURAL	0.	606.	72.	821.	834.	257.	492.	1231.	4313.
Total	582.	970.	125.	1022.	966.	712.	649.	1847.	6873.

Average Annual Growth Rates 1979-2000

URBAN	5.53%	10.22%	6.67%	6.53%	7.44%	7.89%	9.36%	10.41%	7.84%
RURAL	0.0%	1.92%	1.56%	3.33%	3.95%	2.41%	2.58%	4.55%	3.33%
Total	5.53%	3.69%	3.11%	3.81%	4.30%	5.14%	3.55%	5.84%	4.56%

Economic Growth and Distribution Assumptions

The LEAP system requires that activity levels associated with each end-use be projected separately and that urban and rural income distributions be specified. The general procedure used in developing projections is to key activity growth to one of a number of principal demographic and economic variables. These variables, along with their projected growth rates, are summarized in Table 5.4. Although it would have been useful to take a broader measure than GDP growth rate to project change, no such statistical series that is available for Kenya can be used with confidence. Furthermore, in building an end-use analysis, an effort that requires the introduction of a new statistical base, it was felt that the work would become too unwieldy if new economic forecasting methods were introduced. In particular, efforts were made to utilise input-output models but this was abandoned because of lack of time series data and the difficulty of result interpretation which applies even to the First World studies.

Future income distribution fractions are summarized in Table 5.5. Current income distribution curves from both urban and rural households were constructed on the basis of a study undertaken under the auspices of the World Bank. (18) These distribution curves were then advanced at an annual growth rate of 1.6 per cent. (When combined with the different rural/urban absolute level of income and the urban migration pattern, this yields an overall per capita income growth of 2 per cent p.a.).

As noted above, given these underlying demographic and economic assumptions, various end-use activity levels were projected into the future by keying them to these growth rates as appropriate. For example, it was assumed that the number of informal urban establishments would grow at the same rate as urban population. However, one major exception to this procedure should be noted: future growth rates for each modern industrial sector were derived directly from 1978-82 projections, associated with the Five Year Development Plan. However, in light of the overall performance to date which falls short of these projections, a discount factor of 3 per cent was applied to each sector. Projections for selected Base Case activity measures are presented in Table 5.6 below.

Expansion of Agriculture

The rapid population increase expected during the 1980-2000 period will put a heavy burden on the use of the limited areas of productive land in Kenya. The combined national objectives of increased nutritional intake and self-sufficiency in food can be achieved only by a massive expansion of agricultural production. Such expansion can occur as a result of both intensification,

Table 5.4

SUMMARY OF BASE CASE DEMOGRAPHIC AND ECONOMIC GROWTH ASSUMPTIONS

Variable Name	1980 Base Value	1990 Value	2000 Value	Average Annual Growth
. Population - Total (Millions)	16.00	23.87	33.96	3.84%
. Population - Urban (Millions)	2.53	5.59	10.24	7.24%
. Population - Rural (Millions)	13.45	18.29	23.72	2.88%
. Persons Per Household - Total	5.65	5.28	4.94	-0.67%
. Persons Per Household - Urban	4.38	4.19	4.00	-0.45%
. Persons Per Household - Rural	5.98	5.74	5.50	-0.42%
. Gross Domestic Product K£ x 10^6	1963.84	3451.14	6064.84	5.80%
. Gross Domestic Product Per Capita K£	122.86	144.58	178.58	1.89%

Table 5.5

SUMMARY OF BASE CASE INCOME DISTRIBUTIONS

Variable	Base Year Fraction	1990 Fraction	2000 Fraction
Urban			
Income Group 1	0.05	0.07	0.08
Income Group 2	0.23	0.26	0.28
Income Group 3	0.26	0.26	0.27
Income Group 4	0.34	0.31	0.30
Income Group 5	0.12	0.10	0.08
Rural			
Income Group 1	0.16	0.19	0.22
Income Group 2	0.50	0.51	0.51
Income Group 3	0.35	0.30	0.27

Table 5.6

SUMMARY OF BASE CASE PROJECTIONS FOR LEAP ACTIVITY MEASURES

vity Measure	Units	Base Year Value	1990 Value	2000 Value	Basis For Projection
Urban Households	Million Hh.	0.578	1.334	2.561	See Text.
Rural Households	Million Hh.	2.251	3.188	4.313	"
Agricultural	Million Ha.	2.95	3.79	4.63	"
Informal Industrial Activity, Urban	Number of Firms	13.262	29.262	53.629	Urban Population
Informal Industrial Activity, Rural	Rural Population, Million Pers.	13.452	18.291	23.720	Rural Population
Large Industrial Activity:					
Food	GDP Originating Million 1980 K£	106.30	163.41	251.47	Schipper (Technical Vol)
Textiles	"	31.30	79.03	199.54	"
Paper	"	21.90	35.33	56.98	"
Rubber	"	12.40	68.93	170.39	"
Chemicals	"	30.30	71.73	169.82	"
Clay/Glass	"	1.20	2.55	5.40	"
Non Metallic (Cement)	"	9.80	21.16	45.68	"
Metal Products	"	25.00	59.19	140.12	"
Transport Equipment.	"	14.30	37.09	96.20	"
Construction	"	94.30	165.71	291.22	GDP
Other Industry	"	128.90	226.51	398.08	"
Transportation:					
Auto & Station Wagon	Billion Vehicle Km	3.48	6.12	10.75	National Population
Pickups	"	0.907	1.896	2.806	"
Lorries & Trucks	"	0.58	1.01	1.78	GDP
Buses/Coaches	"	0.20	0.31	0.42	National Population
Minibuses	"	0.13	0.23	0.28	BDP
Rail-Passenger	Billion Passenger Km	1.71	2.98	5.25	GDP
Rail-Freight	Billion Tonne Km	1.97	3.44	6.09	"
Air-Commercial	Thousand Flights	33.44	58.17	102.72	"
Pipeline	Million cu.m^3	1.37	1.37	1.37	Assumed Constant
Steamships	Million Freight Tons	5.92	10.36	18.29	GDP
Commercial:					
Schools/Hospitals	Relative Activity Ratio to Base Year	1.00	1.49	2.12	National Population
Offices/Other Serv.	"	1.00	2.21	4.04	Urban Population
Hotels (1000 beds)	Available Beds	24.60	50.00	102.00	Dev. Plan. Projection (7.4%)
Small Consumers	Relative Activity Ratio to Base Year	1.00	1.00	1.00	Assumed Constant

that is, increased productivity of land under cultivation, and extension of cultivation into new land. These objectives themselves compete with yet another national objective, increased production for export. The foreign exchange earnings from agricultural exports such as coffee and tea are important in stimulating the economy as a whole, purchasing needed capital goods and fuel, and in the process of expanding agriculture itself.

In the present study a number of assumptions are made in the Base Case treatment of the agricultural sector. While the focus here is not on agriculture itself, it is necessary to undertake this exercise for two reasons: first, to complete the picture of the Kenyan economy during the period of interest, and second, to identify a consistent set of land use changes that would occur over this period, especially insofar as these affect or constrain energy requirements and wood resource availability. Expansion of agriculture could reduce the scope for certain forms of wood production schemes even as it increases the demand for wood (e.g. for crop drying). The figures used for these projections reflect the policy of the Government of Kenya. It should be noted however, that there is a general per capita decline in food production throughout sub Saharan Africa. The agricultural projections, therefore, are over-optimistic.

It is assumed here that production of export crops will be increased by expanding the land devoted to these crops by 50 per cent over the next twenty years. This will be achieved by bringing uncropped high potential land into production. No increase in productivity is assumed for this category as modern techniques are already in wide use and additional production could be on less productive land. The Food Policy Paper has identified some problems, such as soil erosion, associated with intensive cultivation of some export crops in the past. Accordingly, about 320 thousand hectares will be converted to this use by the year 2000. Food production for domestic consumption is assumed to increase in two ways. First, as identified in the Food Policy Paper greater productivity will be sought through intercropping, multiple cropping, agroforestry, and increased fertilizer, water, mechanical and other inputs, and extension services. While the precise mix of appropriate programmes and techniques is yet to be determined, it is assumed here that a productivity increase of 50 per cent will be achieved by the year 2000. This would still leave the nation far short of food self-sufficiency. Thus, a massive increase in land under food crops is assumed. On a province-by-province basis, once new land allocated to export crops is estimated, and taking grazing requirements into account, the remaining usable uncropped high and medium potential agricultural land is assumed to be converted to food production over the 1980-2000 period. Of course, in addition to food crops, meat and dairy production would have to increase substantially to meet growing food requirements. Thus, the approaches identified in the Food Policy Paper, e.g. improved animal husbandry practices, as well as increased use of rangelands would be required.

The assumptions embodied in the Base Case treatment of agriculture are summarized below in Table 5.7.

The detailed provincial breakdowns and further discussion are presented later. Here it is useful to note that the principal expansion occurs in Rift Valley province (1 million hectares food, 0.32 million hectares export crops), and Coast province (0.32 million additional hectares for food production). Further scope for increased agricultural output could occur if uncropped areas in medium potential land, e.g. rangeland in Coast province and some of the semi-arid lands of Eastern province, were brought into production.

Future End-Use Demand

Tables 5.8, 5.9 and 5.10 below report Base Case projections of selected end-use demands. Discussion of subsector and end-use categories were presented in Chapter 3.

Demand on Energy Resources

The future requirements on primary energy resources are linked to the end-use demands just discussed by a series of conversion processes. A schemata of the major linkages is shown in Figure 5.2.

The long range Base Case projections for the conversion processes themselves (electricity, generation, charcoal production, and oil refining) are discussed below followed by a summary of projected energy resource requirements.

Conversions

The Base Case projections of electrical generation are summarized in Table 5.11. The expansion of capacity for hydro, geothermal and combustion turbines is taken at the planned potential targets. Oil steam is assumed to make up the additional generation requirements. Electricity demand is projected to grow at 6.7 per cent which would, in the absence of conservation efforts or use of non-conventional fuels for generation, require an increase of over 1,100 MW by the end of the century.

The projections include additions by the year 2000 as follows: Hydro Electric (550 MW), Geothermal (100 MW) and Oil Steam (486 MW). Retirement of all diesel generators is also assumed. Of the hydro construction planned, 220 MW are associated with the Tana watershed and 230 MW with other rivers. The latter includes the ambitious Turkwel Gorge project, which is planned to yield 60 MW of firm power out of a total capacity of 100 MW.

Table 5.7

NATIONAL AGRICULTURAL GROWTH - BASE CASE

	Present Land (10^6 Ha.)	Land Added By 2000 (10^6 Ha.)	Productivity Increase By 2000
Food Crops	2.30	1.36	51%
Export Crops	.65	.32	None
Total	2.95	1.68	

Table 5.8

SELECTED BASE CASE END-USE FORECASTS - URBAN HOUSEHOLDS (PJ)

Subsector	End-Use	Fuel	1980	1990	2000
				Demand	
Income Group 1	Cooking, Water Heating, Space Heating	Wood	.58	1.88	4.12
		Charcoal	.23	.76	1.66
		Kerosene	-	-	.01
	Lighting	Kerosene	.08	.26	.57
	Other	Charcoal	.05	.17	.38
Income Group 2	Cooking, Water Heating, Space Heating	Wood	1.07	2.79	5.78
		Charcoal	2.37	6.18	12.77
		Kerosene	.26	.67	1.38
	Lighting	Kerosene	.49	1.27	2.63
		Electricity	-	.02	.02
	Other	Charcoal	.32	.83	1.71
Income Group 3	Cooking, Water Heating, Space Heating	Wood	.89	2.04	4.08
		Charcoal	3.42	7.88	15.71
		Kerosene	.41	.95	1.89
	Lighting	Kerosene	.56	1.29	2.58
		Electricity	.03	.06	.12
	Other	Charcoal	.45	1.04	2.07
		Electricity	.04	.11	.22
Income Group 4	Cooking, Water Heating, Space Heating	Wood	.44	.92	1.71
		Charcoal	4.11	8.66	16.08
		Kerosene	.93	1.96	3.63
		Electricity	.08	.16	.30
	Lighting	Kerosene	.56	1.18	2.19
		Electricity	.17	.35	.65
	Other	Charcoal	.70	1.46	2.72
		Electricity	.37	.78	1.45
Income Group 5	Cooking, Water Heating, Space Heating	Wood	.05	.10	.15
		Charcoal	.87	1.68	2.58
		Kerosene	.36	.69	1.06
		Electricity	.66	1.28	1.96
	Lighting	Kerosene	.04	.08	.12
		Electricity	.28	.54	.82
	Other	Charcoal	.14	.27	.41
		Electricity	.45	.86	1.31

Table 5-9

SELECTED BASE CASE END-USE FORECASTS - RURAL HOUSEHOLDS   (PJ)

Subsector	End-Use	Fuel	1980	1990	2000
Income Group 1	Cooking	Woodfuel	21.90	36.83	57.70
		Charcoal	0.10	0.17	0.26
		Biomass/Residue	0.48	0.81	1.26
		Kerosene	0.02	0.04	0.06
		Maize	0.56	0.95	1.48
	Heating	Woodfuel	2.82	4.74	7.42
		Charcoal	0.07	0.13	0.20
		Biomass/Residue	0.22	0.36	0.57
		Maize	0.02	0.03	0.04
	Lighting	Kerosene	0.44	0.75	1.17
Income Group 2	Cooking	Woodfuel	70.21	101.42	137.21
		Charcoal	3.17	4.58	6.19
		Biomass/Residue	1.05	1.51	2.05
		Kerosene	0.27	0.39	0.52
		Maize	2.91	4.20	5.68
	Heating	Woodfuel	7.28	10.52	14.24
		Charcoal	0.35	0.51	0.69
		Biomass/Residue	0.33	0.48	0.65
		Maize	0.18	0.26	0.36
	Lighting	Kerosene	1.75	2.53	3.42
Income Group 3	Cooking	Woodfuel	42.25	51.29	62.45
		Charcoal	4.37	5.30	6.46
		Biomass/Residue	0.51	0.62	0.75
		Kerosene	0.22	0.27	0.32
		Maize	2.50	3.04	3.70
	Heating	Woodfuel	6.11	7.41	9.02
		Charcoal	1.18	1.43	1.75
		Biomass/Residue	0.23	0.28	0.34
	Lighting	Kerosene	1.49	1.81	2.20

Table 5.10

SELECTED BASE CASE END-USE FORECASTS - OTHER SECTORS   (PJ)

Sector	End-Use	Fuel	1980	Demand 1990	2000
Agriculture	All	Gasoline	1.02	1.31	1.60
		Diesel	6.63	8.51	10.40
		Electricity	0.59	1.11	2.05
Informal Industry Urban	Process Heat	Wood	.21	.45	.83
		Charcoal	.47	1.03	1.90
	Cooking	Wood	.17	.38	.70
		Charcoal	.40	.89	1.62
Informal Industry Rural	Brewing	Wood	14.39	19.57	25.38
	Pottery/Brick	Wood	.79	1.08	1.40
	Blacksmith	Charcoal	.77	1.04	1.35
	Curing	Wood	.32	.44	.57
	Drying	Wood	.48	.66	.85
	Shops	Wood	3.20	4.35	5.65
		Charcoal	.77	1.04	1.35
	Poles	Wood	6.72	9.14	11.86
	Tobacco	Wood	.48	.66	.85
	Baking	Wood	1.76	2.40	3.11
	Eating Places	Wood	2.25	3.05	3.96
		Charcoal	.54	.73	.95
Large Industry	Process	Bottled Gas	0.17	0.36	0.74
		Kerosene	0.91	1.87	3.87
		Residual Oil	17.92	36.65	75.47
		Electricity	1.77	3.79	8.10
	Feedstock	Wood	6.30	10.75	18.38
	Miscellaneous	Wood	17.44	30.61	53.74
Transportation	Private Vehicles	Gasoline	16.62	30.73	51.39
	Trucks	Diesel	9.80	17.07	30.08
	Buses	Diesel	2.58	4.00	5.42
	Minibus	Gasoline	.72	1.29	1.57
	Rail	Oil	2.52	4.40	7.77
	Air (Internal & External)	Jet Fuel	11.89	20.68	36.52
Commercial Schools/Hospitals	Space Conditioning, Lighting	Wood	1.60	2.38	3.39
		Charcoal	0.39	0.58	0.82
		Bottled Gas	.07	.11	.16
		Oil	.17	.25	.36
		Electricity	.13	.19	.27
Offices	Lighting	Electricity	.78	1.73	3.17
		Oil	.08	.18	.33
Hotels	Lighting	Oil	.32	.64	1.31
		Electricity	.16	.32	.65
		Bottled Gas	.14	.28	.57
		Kerosene	.06	.11	.23
Small Consumers	All	Electricity	.24	.24	.24

Figure 5.2 Schema of Energy Flows

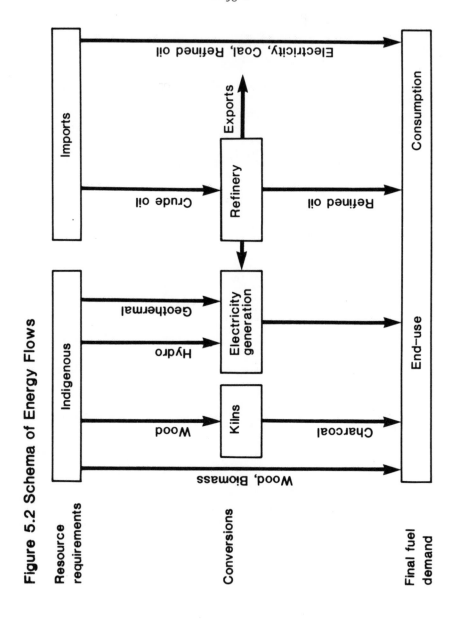

Table 5.11

ELECTRICAL GENERATION (MW CAPACITY & GWh GENERATION)
BASE YEAR PROJECTIONS

Type/Year	1980	1985	1990	1995	2000
Uganda Imports					
Capacity (MW)	30.	30.	30.	30.	30.
Generat. (GWh)	333.	237.	237.	237.	237.
Hydro Power					
Capacity (MW)	300.	450.	600.	725.	850.
Generat. (GWh)	1100.	1971.	2628.	3176.	3723.
Geothermal					
Capacity (MW)	0.	23.	45.	73.	100.
Generat. (GWh)	0.	59.	118.	191.	263.
Combust Turbines					
Capacity (MW)	22.	22.	22.	22.	22.
Generat. (GWh)	26.	19.	19.	19.	19.
Diesel					
Capacity (MW)	19.	10.	0.	0.	0.
Generat. (GWh)	26.	8.	0.	0.	0.
Oil Steam					
Capacity (MW)	93.	110.	152.	373.	579.
Generat. (GWh)	349.	481.	667.	1634.	2537.
Total Electric					
Capacity (MW)	464.	644.	849.	1222.	1581.
Generat. (GWh)	1835.	2775.	3669.	5255.	6779.

The Base Case does not assume operation of two 15 MW geothermal facilities at Olkaria Valley. This project is presently underway. Additional sites in the Olkaria area have yielded estimates of an additional 144 MW of exploitable potential. However, we have not assumed that all these will come on-line in our Base Case. Further, additional geothermal areas with 326 MW of exploitable potential have been identified south of Lake Bogoria and in the Eburna area, north of Lake Naivasha. High temperatures have also been found in shallow boreholes near Lake Elementeita, Lake Magadi and Lake Baringo. Indeed, geothermal generation figures to be a major source of future energy. However, insofar as the exact magnitude of this development is yet uncertain, the prudent course is to assume that future developments are limited to the Olkaria facility presently under construction.

Estimated retirements are based on the standard practice in electrical systems planning of taking the economic lives of generating facilities as 50, 25, and 15 years for hydro, oil-steam, gas turbine and diesel plants respectively. EAP&L, for instance, proposed in 1978 the retirement of 82.8 MW of capacity by 1986. The Base Case shows only the net increment in each class of plant, equal to new plant less retirements.

Capacity factors (average to maximum power output) and efficiencies for each type of plant are assumed to remain at constant levels over the forecast horizon. Conversion efficiencies for oil-fired facilities were reported in Table 3.14 from data provided in the National Development Plan. Capacity factors are a function of system operation and both planned and forced outages. For instance, the irregular rainfall pattern characteristic of the Tana watershed accounts for the estimate of 35 per cent for the capacity factor associated with hydroelectric generation.

Prospects for non-conventional sources of electric generation are discussed in Chapter 6. None are found to have adequately passed the tests of availability, feasibility, and cost-effectiveness at this time to warrant inclusion in a Policy Case planning programme.

We turn now to the conversion of wood to charcoal. Traditional earthen kilns, from which almost all charcoal used in Kenya is produced, in the absence of major policy initiatives (the Base Case), are assumed to remain dominant throughout the remainder of the century. The relatively low energy efficiency of this process (about 24 per cent), or about one third of the maximum (1), makes this a high priority problem as charcoal requirements increase rapidly over the next two decades. More efficient kilns, however, are costly and require economies of scale in operation that are not satisfied by the current practices of charcoal production, done largely by small independent producers using wood from isolated trees and scrubs on rangelands and savannah. Thus, despite growing charcoal requirements, major introduction of more efficient kilns would most likely have to be associated with more concentrated production from large fuelwood plantations or forests.

The final conversion process to be considered here is the production of petroleum products to meet final consumption requirements. Base Case projections are summarized in Table 5.12. The table includes a summary of internal uses where we see the rapid overall growth rate in internal demand for petroleum products (6.2 per cent p.a.) driven by the large industry, transportation, and electricity generation sectors. The rapid increase in imported refined oil reflects the Base Case assumption of non-expansion of the refinery capacity. Were refinery capacity added, then of course imported crude would substitute. Additionally, no contribution from domestic crude is included in the Base Case projections. Until there is a positive identification of domestically available oil resources which can be economically extracted, planning prudence dictates that no such resources be assumed.

(1) The maximum theoretical conversion percentage is 83 on an energy for energy basis. This is equivalent to a conversion percentage of 44 on a (bone dry) weight for weight ratio which represents the maximum amount of fixed carbon in cellulose.

Forecast of Requirements

Future Base Case requirements, taking account of projected end-use demand-use demand and conversion/distribution losses is summarized in Table 5.13.

Here we see the anticipation of rapid growth in Base Case energy source requirements of 4.9 per cent p.a.*, led by growth in total oil requirements at 4.0 per cent p.a. and continued substantial growth in wood requirements at 4.6 per cent p.a. Increases in wood used for charcoal production is notable, growing at 6.0 per cent p.a. and increasing its share of total wood requirements from 33 per cent to 43 per cent over the study timeframe.

The requirements for wood and oil are re-expressed in physical terms in Table 5.14. Note that the national wood requirement is equivalent to about 1.3 M^3 per capita in 1980 (converted at 1.4 M^3 per tonne for air-dried wood). This independently derived estimate is consistent with many aggregate rule-of-thumb estimates in the literature. The figure actually increases in the projections (1.5 M^3 p.c. in 2000) due to the increased usage of charcoal accompanying the urbanization process with concomitant conversion losses in charcoal production.

*p.a. = per annum

Table 5.12

BASE CASE SOURCES AND USES OF OIL (MILLION BARRELS)

	1980	1985	1990	1995	2000
Sources					
Imported Crude	20.7	24.1	26.3	26.3	26.3
Domestic Crude	0.0	0.0	0.0	0.0	0.0
Imported Refined	1.5	2.1	4.2	14.2	24.1
Total Sources	22.2	26.3	30.5	40.5	50.4
Uses					
Internal Demand					
Urban Household	.6	1.0	1.3	2.0	2.6
Rural Household	.7	.8	.9	1.1	1.2
Agriculture	1.2	1.4	1.6	1.7	1.9
Informal Ind.Urban	0	0	0	0	0
Informal Ind.Rural	0	0	0	0	0
Large Industry	3.0	4.6	6.2	9.5	12.8
Transportation	7.3	10.0	12.8	17.3	21.8
Commercial	.2	.2	.3	.4	.5
Elec.Generation	1.8	2.5	3.2	6.1	8.7
Total Internal	14.8	20.5	26.3	38.1	49.6
Exported Refined	6.8	5.1	3.4	1.7	0.0
Refinery Loss	0.6	0.7	0.8	0.8	0.8
Exported Crude	0.0	0.0	0.0	0.0	0.0
Total Used	22.2	26.3	30.5	40.5	50.4
Refinery Capacity	26.3	26.3	26.3	26.3	26.3

Table 5.13

PROJECTED ENERGY RESOURCE REQUIREMENTS TO MEET KENYA DEMAND (PJ)

Source	1980	1985	1990	1995	2000
Total Wood	332.6	430.7	527.7	669.0	810.9
Wood For Firewood	209.1	255.6	302.2	362.7	423.6
Wood For Charcoal	111.0	158.1	204.1	277.3	350.7
Wood For Indust.	12.5	17.0	21.4	29.0	36.6
Total Oil	136.9	162.3	188.4	250.2	311.0
Refined Oil	9.3	13.3	26.1	87.9	148.7
Imported Crude	127.6	149.0	162.3	162.3	162.3
Hydro	4.0	7.1	9.5	11.4	13.4
Geothermal	0.0	0.5	1.1	1.7	2.4
Elec. Imports	1.2	0.9	0.9	0.9	0.9
Coal	1.4	2.2	3.0	4.7	6.4
Biomass	9.3	11.2	13.0	15.2	17.5
Solar	0.0	0.0	0.0	0.0	0.0
Total Sources:	485.4	614.9	743.6	953.1	1162.4

Table 5.14

WOOD AND OIL REQUIREMENTS TO MEET KENYAN DEMAND

	1980	1985	1990	1995	2000
Total Wood	20.4	26.4	32.3	41.1	49.7
Wood For Fuel Million Tonnes	12.8	15.7	18.5	22.3	26.0
Wood For Charcoal Million Tonnes	6.8	9.7	12.5	17.0	21.5
Wood For Industry Million Tonnes	0.8	1.0	1.3	1.8	2.2
Total Oil	22.2	26.2	30.5	40.5	50.4
Refined Oil Million BBL	1.5	2.1	4.2	14.2	24.1
Imported Crude Million BBL	20.7	24.1	26.3	26.3	26.3

Wood Resource Adequacy

As we have seen, wood resources for meeting fuelwood, charcoal, rural poles and industrial/construction demands are derived from both annual production (or yields) and standing stocks on the various landtypes. The amounts of each type consumed depend on regional supply/demand balances. The accessibility of wood resources is circumscribed by geographic, technological, and socio-economic factors, as described earlier. In instances (particular provinces/landtypes) where demand exceeds annual production of woody biomass a net depletion of standing stocks will occur in the attempt to satisfy demand. There is evidence that this process is already being experienced on a local basis in Kenya. At present some animal waste and crop residue is being used to service rural energy needs. And, at present about 45 per cent of wood resource demand in Kenya, some 9.26 million tonnes, is met by a net reduction in standing stocks.

In assessing wood resource adequacy two principal dimensions of the problem deserve attention. First, is the accessible supply sufficient to meet demand as it increases rapidly, as projected by the Base Case, over the next twenty years? Second, as demand increases to what extent are standing stocks of woody biomass depleted? Associated with this second problem is the potential for soil loss, especially on cultivated agricultural land.

Land Use Projections

A number of changes in land use patterns are expected to occur in Kenya over the next twenty years as a consequence of demographic trends and development objectives. The assumptions made for the purposes of this investigation and the results deriving from these assumptions are summarized in Table 5.15.

First, as discussed above, agricultural land devoted to food production must increase in order that the national food policy goal of self-sufficiency be achieved. Since an overall increase in productivity of 50 per cent has been assumed here, this implies that land under food crops will need to increase from about 2.3 million hectares at present to 3.66 million hectares by the year 2000. This expansion of 1.36 million hectares is assumed to occur in Coast, Rift Valley, and Western provinces where usable uncultivated agricultural land exists. In Rift Valley, 700 thousand hectares of uncultivated land on large farms and 300 thousand hectares from uncultivated land on small farms, both on high potential land, is converted to food production by the end of the century. This is consistent with government resettlement policy to convert uncultivated largeholder lands to smallholder farming. In Coast province 80 thousand hectares of uncultivated high potential land and 240 thousand hectares of rangeland is

Table 5.15

LAND USE CHANGES - BASE CASE 1980/2000 (THOUSANDS OF HECTARES)

Landtype	Central/Nairobi	Coast	Eastern	North-Eastern	Nyanza	Rift Valley	Western	Total
Large Farm Food	15	7/47	10	-	15	160/860	6	213/953
Large Farm Temp.	25	-	6	-	1	115/235	-	147/267
Large Farm Perm.	38	33	13	-	1	48/248	-	133/333
Large Farm Uncv.	256/238	45/5	246	-	12	1698/618	3	2260/1122
Small Farm Food	404	113/393	690	-	424	133/433	323/363	2086/2706
Small Farm Temp.	11	3	13	-	23	4	31	85
Small Farm Perm.	93	97	70	-	17	4	4	285
Small Farm Uncv.	128/91	132/67	902/839	-	664/629	403/16	353/288	2582/1930
Urban Built Env.	13/37	6/25	4/12	2/8	4/22	8/52	2/11	39/167
Rural Built Env.	37/74	45/66	112/197	-	50/67	92/204	31/47	366/655
Parks/Reserves	121	1633	1245	53	35	562	1	3650
Natural Forests	205	118	132	-	3	653	56	1166
Woodlot Exist	4	-	1	-	0	15	1	21
MGD Forest Plnt.	25	2	9	-	1	87	11	135
Savannah Bush	-	3049	3430	6796/6791	-	6795/6792	-	20070/20061
Savannah Grass	-	2398	8061	5839	-	5999	-	22296
Rangeland	12/7	622/368	634/603	-	3	107/102	-	1379/1082

shifted to food production. In Western province 40 thousand hectares of uncultivated high potential land is brought into food production during this period.

It is also probable that some forest land will be converted to agricultural use by the year 2000, maybe about 0.12 million hectares or 10 per cent of the gazetted forest area under trees. Again there are some 0.45 million hectares of gazetted forest land with little or no tree cover, and some, if not the majority of this land will be under (illegal) agriculture. However, food production for self-sufficiency is a priority and more forest land could be given up voluntarily for agriculture provided more intensive forest management is applied to the remaining areas. With better management, unit wood production could at least be doubled, but this will require trained manpower and the introduction of improved techniques.

If some forest land is to be converted to agriculture, it could be made a condition that a certain number of trees be left on the land or new varieties be planted so at least these surrendered areas will be self-sufficient in wood products. Also, this condition could apply to the gazetted forest land that has already been converted to agriculture. Such areas would be demonstration units for agro-forestry techniques and be a positive step to help the rural people produce both more food and fuel.

Land devoted primarily to export crops is assumed to increase by 50 per cent by the end of the century from about 650 thousand hectares to 970 thousand hectares by the year 2000. This is achieved by converting from uncultivated high potential land on large farms in Rift Valley province.

Other land use changes are associated with population increases and the need to expand urban and rural structures and infrastructures to satisfy the living and working requirements of the population. Land devoted to rural and urban built environments (structures, roads, etc.) is therefore expected to grow at rates commensurate with the expansion of these populations. Rural built environment will increase from about 366 thousand hectares to 655 thousand hectares, while urban environment will grow from about 39 thousand hectares to 167 thousand hectares by the end of the century. This expansion will of course differ by province according to province-specific demographic trends. Moreover, in each province expansion of built environment will occur at the expense of other landtypes available for this conversion. The principal landtypes into which urban built environment expands are largeholder and smallholder uncropped lands in high potential areas and rangeland and savannah lands in medium and semi-arid areas. Rural built environment is assumed to expand into uncultivated smallholder lands.

The details of land use changes on a regional and economic basis are presented in the first technical volume. Here they are summarized for the years 1980 and 2000 in Table 5.15, where changes are indicated for the year 2000.

Wood Supply/Demand Relationships

As noted earlier, Kenya is presently in a situation where stocks are being depleted in order to help satisfy fuelwood and charcoal demands. Moreover, the beginning of a shift towards the use of animal waste and crop residue is occurring. The analysis here is not directed towards identifying more local pockets of unsatisfied demand which, to be sure, are already being experienced. The forms in which this is expressed could include: use of non-woody biomass (3 per cent of end-use biomass energy demand), shorter cooking times, more infrequent cooking, and greater care in the use of fuelwood, and fewer social uses.

More serious problems, however, begin to emerge on a national basis by the early 1980s when demand increasingly exceeds wood yield. In a vicious circle, as standing stocks begin to be depleted, yields are further decreased and stock depletion is further accelerated.(19) This is summarized in Table 5.16 and Figure 5.3.

From these results it is apparent that on a national basis a fuelwood crisis is already occurring with respect to net stock depletion, which begins to escalate rapidly after the late 1980s, reaching a staggering 21.62 million tonnes per year by 1995. Stock depletion only begins to abate after 1995 as a consequence of constraints on accessibility. That is, accessible stocks in some provinces become exhausted, leaving the local population without means of obtaining fuelwood. Standing stocks as a whole are expected to decline about 30 per cent over the 1980-2000 period. The depletion of accessible stocks is, of course, much more dramatic, as is evident from the rapid increase in supplies from this source after 1985 followed by a rapid decline after 1995. One should picture much of the remaining stock, not as pristine forest, but as stripped tree trunks.

The other major problem embodied in these results is that wood supply insufficiency begins in the early 1980s, increases steadily through the early 1990s, and expands rapidly into a huge potential shortfall by the end of the century. By 1985 a shortfall of 6.1 million tonnes, about 23 per cent of wood demand, is reached. By 1990 the shortfall will grow to 10.8 million tonnes, or about one third of total demand. Finally, by the year 2000 a shortfall of 32.1 million tonnes is projected, about 65 per cent of wood demand nationally, if prevailing conditions and practices remain unaltered for the remainder of the century.

Table 5.17 summarizes another disturbing result of our analyses. The depletion of standing stocks of woody biomass on cultivated agricultural land is very dramatic. The density of wood stocks on this land decreases from an average of 11.0 tonnes per hectare in 1980 to 5.0 tonnes per hectare in 2000. This 50 per cent reduction could have serious consequences for soil retention and agricultural productivity.

Table 5.16

NATIONAL WOOD RESOURCE SUPPLY/DEMAND RELATIONSHIP IN KENYA
(MILLION OF TONNES)

	1980	1985	1990	1995	2000
Demand	20.41	26.42	32.37	41.04	49.74
Supplied					
From Yields*	11.07	9.41	8.06	6.29	4.97
From Stocks+	9.26	10.94	13.51	21.62	12.16
Shortfall	.08	6.07	10.80	13.13	32.61
Standing Stock	934.82	885.41	829.36	744.49	674.40

* Yields: Net annual production. Only accessible yields service demand.

+ Stocks: Net reduction in accessible standing stocks service demand when demand exceeds accessible yields.

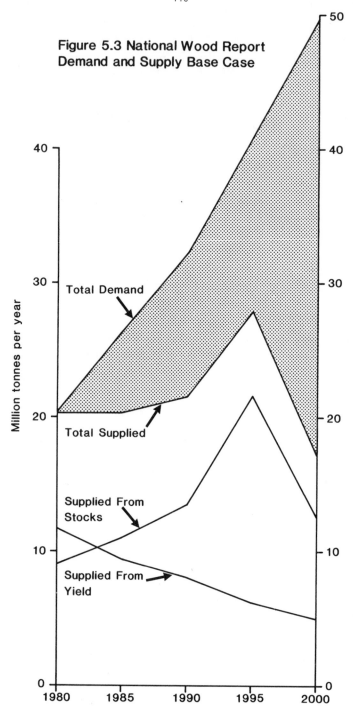

Figure 5.3 National Wood Report Demand and Supply Base Case

Table 5.17

WOOD RESOURCES ON CULTIVATED LAND - BASE CASE

	1980	1985	1990	1995	2000
Stocks (Million Tonnes)	32.51	27.94	27.97	25.34	23.16
Area (Million Hectares)	2.95	3.37	3.79	4.21	4.63
Stocks per area (Tonnes/Hectare)	11.02	8.29	7.38	6.02	5.00
Percent Loss of Wood Density		25	33	45	55

On a regional basis there is great diversity in the
magnitude and timing of wood supply/demand and stock depletion
problems. Some provinces do not experience any shortfalls at all
during the 1980-2000 period. These provinces - Coast, Eastern,
and Northeastern - have rather low population densities on a
province-wide basis. As a result there are adequate accessible
supplies of wood resources to meet demand. However, in order that
demand be met, net offtake of standing stocks would be necessary
in Coast and Eastern provinces, by the mid 1980s. By the end of
the century almost 90 per cent of wood resources supplied in
these two provinces will be derived from standing stocks,
resulting in 32 per cent stock depletion by the year 2000 and
serious reduction in quality of remaining stocks.

Rift Valley province is not expected to incur a shortfall
until the late 1990s. However, to meet demand until then, the
cutting of accessible standing stocks will increase rapidly,
until these are essentially depleted in the mid-1990s. By 1995,
about 12 million tonnes of stocks are cut, roughly 85 per cent of
wood supplied. After this, a rapid increase in the shortfall will
occur, reaching more than 90 per cent by the year 2000. Total
standing stocks decline by over 30 per cent, primarily during the
last five years of the century.

Serious problems can be expected to emerge much earlier in
the densely populated provinces of Central/Nairobi, Nyanza, and
Western. Central/Nairobi is already experiencing substantial
stock cutting, over 60 per cent of supplies, to meet demand. By
1985 accessible stocks begin to be exhausted, and the onset of a
growing supply shortfall will occur in the late 1980s. The
shortfall will reach more than 90 per cent and stocks will have
declined by 30 per cent by the end of the century. More serious
results are found for Nyanza and Western provinces, where at
present about 85 per cent of demand may be met by the net
reduction of accessible standing stocks of woody biomass. Supply
shortfalls in these two provinces will begin during the early to
mid 1980s and will increase to about 100 per cent very rapidly.
More than 50 per cent of standing stocks in Nyanza and more than
35 per cent in Western province will have been removed by the end
of the century.

The regional impacts discussed above are summarized in Table
5.18. There another interesting result emerges. While in 1985 all
of the supply shortfall, about 5.4 million tonnes, occurs in
Nyanza and Western provinces, by the end of the century Rift
Valley and Central/Nairobi incur more than 70 per cent of a much
larger shortfall of 32.61 million tonnes. Moreover, while Coast
and Eastern provinces incur no shortfalls by the year 2000, this
occurs as a result of a steady net depletion of standing stocks.
Thus, these provinces would be expected to incur shortfalls in
the first decades of the 21st century.

Table 5.18

SUMMARY OF REGIONAL SUPPLY/DEMAND RELATIONSHIPS (1980-2000)

	Central/Nairobi	Coast	Eastern	North-Eastern	Nyanza	Rift Valley	Western
Onset of Supply Shortfall	1980	-	1981-82	-	1982-85	1980	1982-85
Onset of Net Stock Depletion	1980	1980	1980	-	1980	1980	1980
Shortfall as Percent of Demand							
1985	1	-	-	-	100	1	99
2000	90	-	-	-	100	91	98
Net Stock Depletion as Percent of Wood Supply							
1980	63	17	25	-	85	34	87
1985	84	41	43	-	-	56	-
2000	-	89	89	-	-	-	-
Cumulative Stock Depletion (Percent)							
1985	21	3	3	-	51	5	35
2000	28	32	32	-	52	39	35
Contribution to National Shortfall (Percent)							
1985	1	-	-	-	48	2	49
2000	17	-	-	-	13	53	17
Contribution to National Shortfall (Million Tonnes)							
1985	-	-	-	-	2.9	.1	3.0
2000	5.5	-	-	-	4.3	17.3	5.5

The Coming Energy Crisis

The results of the Base Case analysis demonstrate that a deepening energy crisis, beginning in the early 1980s, will befall Kenya if no programmatic effort is undertaken to avoid it. The two poles of this crisis are associated with oil and wood requirements and the consequences of attempting to satisfy them under prevailing conditions.

In the case of oil requirements to meet Kenyan demand, expected to grow from 13.1 million barrels imported in 1980 to 41.5 million barrels by the year 2000, the foreign exchange requirements necessary to sustain growth in the oil based (i.e. commercial) sector of the economy will be massive. Even if oil prices do not continue to escalate as rapidly as they have in the past, the prospect for a worsening deficit in Kenya's balance of payments looms very large. Kenya has already experienced some consequences of balance of payments problems.(20) The possibility of a serious slowdown of economic growth, so essential for national development and improved conditions of life for its people, threatens Kenya's future.

An illustration of the scale of the oil-import burden facing Kenya may be instructive. Even if one makes the unreasonable assumption that oil prices do not increase from current values (about 300 KShs per barrel), the oil import bill would exceed total current export earnings by 1990. If one assumes a more realistic 10 per cent annual escalation rate in the price of oil, the oil import bill would equal twice current export earnings by 1990. This suggests that under Base Case conditions, the Kenyan economy and basic development goals will be placed under serious stress.

The expected increase in wood resource requirements, from 20 million tonnes in 1980 to 49 million tonnes by the year 2000, cannot be met if current conditions and practices remain unchanged. A growing shortfall, reaching 10 million tonnes by 1990 and 33 million tonnes by 2000, would cause serious problems and dislocations in Kenya's rural economy. These problems would embody economic, social, demographic, and ecological dimensions that could dramatically undermine development and the standard of living of the Kenyan people.

It is apparent from these results that the Kenyan economy, and the rural sector in particular, cannot endure the massive shortfalls in wood-resource supplies that may occur over the next two decades of this century. Almost 25 per cent of national demand for wood will go unmet by 1990, and more than 65 per cent by 2000, if no major policy affecting the supply/demand configuration is undertaken very soon.

The problems that could emerge as a consequence of this situation are deep and manifold, especially in the rural areas. If no other major fuel becomes available in these areas, the population would have to reduce or radically change its patterns of consumption. The use of wood for social and other household and communal activities would probably have to be curtailed. Reduced cooking times, more infrequent meals, and changes in dietary patterns (e.g. from maize and beans to the less balanced ugali) could reduce nutrition and the level of health. Shifting from wood to dung and crop residues could also have deleterious effects. Cooking directly with dung could increase the bacteriological intake, thus increasing disease potential. Removal of animal waste and crop residues from the soil cycle could deplete the soil of nutrients, thus reducing agricultural productivity. This will probably hit earliest and hardest for the poorest subsistence farmers, in Western and Nyanza provinces. The larger more prosperous farmers could have surpluses of wood at least in the earliest years, while small subsistence farmers would face shortages. These surpluses could be kept from local markets by private management of offtake to avoid soil loss and declines in productivity. As a consequence of privatization, then, the poorer farmers could be beset by increasingly inadequate supplies of fuelwood. In this study, however, we have assumed that as wood resources become more scarce these supplies will reach markets. This could imply increasing commoditization of fuelwood in the rural sector, perhaps cutting the poorest segments of the population from access to fuelwood. If alternative fuels such as paraffin are substituted in an attempt to close the gap, these could be either too expensive or not plentiful enough to satisfy rural demand.

As farm and local supplies of fuelwood become exhausted, increasing amounts of time from an already burdened household labour-time budget will be expended in search of adequate supplies with decreasing prospects for satisfaction of these needs. This could have the consequence of keeping family sizes larger and impelling increased migration to the towns and cities.

At the same time, as shown earlier, the depletion of wood stocks on cultivated agricultural land can be expected to occur rapidly. As has been pointed out in the Food Policy Paper (21), and by Dunn (22), the agricultural sector in Kenya is already facing problems of soil erosion arising from expansion of both subsistence farming and export crop production. The depletion of wood resources on these lands, for fuelwood purposes, could exacerbate these problems. Decreases in land productivity that could ensue would lead to further destabilization of the rural sector and increased rates of urbanization.

The potential for severe economic deterioration in rural Kenya attendant upon fuelwood shortages and wood resource depletion could not be confined to the rural sector alone. Supplies of food in general would be expected to decline relative to requirements, and the earnings from agricultural exports could suffer. Moreover, the growth in economic demand and savings that could help spur the economy as a whole might not materialize. The continued economic, social, demographic, and ecological consequences of the devolution of the rural sector that could occur as a consequence of the fuelwood crisis in Kenya would have damaging impacts on the Kenyan society and economy as a whole.

CHAPTER 6. ENERGY STRATEGY OPTIONS

The Base Case projection, a trend-based evolution of energy
supplies and demands under business-as-usual conditions, is not
an acceptable or even a realistic future for Kenya. To avoid the
parallel energy crises emerging in the rural and modern
economies, an unprecedented energy planning effort is required.
It is the purpose of this section to review the major
strategic options available to Kenya for the next two decades and
assess those with greatest promise. This will provide background
and guidance for the creation of concrete initial targets for
energy development policy in the Policy Case projections reported
in Chapter 7.

Increase Wood Supplies

The rapidly escalating demand for wood resources in Kenya
calls for major efforts on the supply-side, especially if end-use
and conversion-technology efficiency improvements are not, by
themselves, sufficient to eliminate potential shortfalls. Large
scale wood resource enhancement policies are necessary if a
number of serious consequences of resource shortfall are to be
avoided.
The consequences of wood resource shortages could include
tree cover removal, especially in cultivated agricultural lands,
where deterioration of soil quality could result. In addition,
diminished food production and decreased nutritional and health
levels could result from soil deterioration, increased fuelwood
gathering time, and decreased cooking times. Requirements for
cooking fuel could go unmet in many areas and shifts to the use
of dung and crop residues could exacerbate soil quality and
health problems. Conditions of life in rural Kenya especially
could decline and devolution of the rural sector could arise.
Impacts on the rural poor would be particularly severe. Export
crop production could be adversely affected as well.
Government plans for overall economic development,
especially the objectives of increased food production and a
strengthened rural economy and infrastructure, would be severely
undermined by fuelwood supply shortages. The problem could turn
from one of economic and social gains to one of sheer survival.
A national programme to augment the supply of wood resources
in Kenya, therefore, entails a challenge and an opportunity both
to avoid crisis and to articulate a crucial component of
development strategy for the nation. Both food and energy
requirements dictate that sufficient indigenous resources and
associated technologies be developed. This is especially
important since the high, and generally rising, cost of fossil
fuels, would, in the face of serious balance of payments

problems, impede development by constricting (or even eliminating) domestic capital formation. Enhancing the domestic wood resource base could establish the conditions upon which a sustainable energy future, consistent with development objectives, can be built.

The wood resource enhancement policies that have been identified by this study as attractive options for Kenya include:

a) AGROFORESTRY,
b) REPLANTED FORESTS,
c) PERIURBAN PLANTATIONS,
d) INDUSTRIAL FORESTS, and
e) MANAGEMENT OF NATURAL FORESTS.

A vital and necessary part of all these policies is improved management, worker training, and introduction of new techniques. The proposed second university, with an expanded faculty of forestry, is an essential prerequisite to the success of such proposals. Among these options, both periurban and industrial plantations would require that land be reallocated from some other current or potential future use, e.g. uncropped agricultural areas. The various forest schemes would require no new land use allocation and therefore would not directly compete with or constrain alternative land-use strategies. Agroforestry falls between these two extremes. While agroforestry would allow the production of wood resources in conjunction with crops on both existing and new agricultural lands, it could compete somewhat with agricultural production, if more intensive cultivation is desired.

Each of these schemes has specific characteristics that affect its potential advantages and role in an overall wood resource policy plan. These include physical characteristics, location, timing, costs, and implementation experience. Each would require specific institutional, educational, labour, and financial conditions and arrangements in order that its potential be realized. In this section some of the major characteristics of these schemes and their physical potential for augmenting the wood resource base are summarized. Maximum targets for each of these schemes on a national and regional basis have been set. While the specific targets to be embodied in a policy scenario must be based upon the configuration of both national and regional wood requirements, and the imbalances discussed earlier, it is useful to begin by examining these targets.

Agroforestry

Agroforestry schemes - the combined farming of selected tree species and existing crops and livestock - have been identified as appropriate for increasing Kenya's wood resources. There are a

number of advantages to such schemes. First, present estimates
demonstrate that, on a national basis, 42 per cent of total
woodfuel demand is supplied by trees on agricultural land. Within
any given region, these figures may be even higher, emphasizing
the fact that most wood supplies are located on farms, where the
rural population lives and works. It is precisely in the high
potential areas of Kenya where high populations place the
greatest demands, and therefore the greatest pressure, on the
wood resources.

Second, present fuelwood gathering techniques concentrate on
wood that is small in diameter. This practice offers the
possibility of developing short rotation "energy trees", which
could be easily integrated into local farming systems.

Third, rather than depleting local resources under
conditions of wood scarcity, which could potentially lead to soil
erosion and declining agricultural output, agroforestry could
serve to improve overall agricultural productivity.
Nitrogen-fixing trees increase the fertility of the soil, while
leaves and pods supply food and fodder. In addition, the rural
household labour time budget, strained by fuelwood gathering
requirements, could be relieved of this burden, thus liberating
the rural population for greater productive work and leisure
time, educational, and social activities. Also, inasmuch as
increased family size is associated with fuelwood gathering
requirements, such pressure could be relieved. Finally, the
possibility emerges for farmers to earn additional income by
sales of wood and charcoal.

Agroforestry schemes have potential negative aspects as
well, some of which are directly related to their advantages.
First, while the competition for land use between food and fuel
is not immediate, it could still nonetheless emerge. As we have
seen, Kenya's rapid population growth combined with the national
objective of food self-sufficiency, increased nutritional
consumption, and maintenance (indeed expansion) of agricultural
exports, necessitates a substantial increase in agricultural
output. (Food output grows at 4.6 per cent/year in the Base
Case.) This will entail both expansion into presently uncropped
lands and increased agricultural productivity. Increased
productivity could be based on additional fuel, fertilizer,
irrigation and mechanization inputs. But other methods
identified, increasing the productivity of land by intercropping
and multiple cropping techniques, could constrain the potential
for agroforestry and vice-versa. Moreover, as expansion into
relatively scarce uncropped arable lands will be necessary,
competition between food and fuel production could emerge. A
problem could also arise due to income inequality and land tenure
constraints. Agroforestry, and the resources and incomes that
could be derived from it, may not be evenly accessible to the
rural population as a whole. In addition, the increased
commoditization of fuelwood could make it difficult for poorer

segments of the rural population to meet their needs. Greater income disparity could emerge in rural Kenya unless programmatic attention is given to these problems.

The potential advantages and problems associated with agroforestry must be weighed in elaborating and carrying out this component of a national wood resource programme. Such planning must be consistent with other national goals such as food self-sufficiency and increased income equity. The opportunity for introducing agroforestry will depend upon the acknowledgement of the fact that farmers are currently producing food and fuel themselves. To optimize this production, assistance is needed in the development of systems which integrate agriculture and forestry. The role of training and extension services will be crucial in this process.

The species identified for agroforestry in Kenya include, among others, Acacia mangium, Alnus nepalensis, Calliandra calothyrsus, Grevillea robusta, Leucaena leucocephala, and Sesbania grandiflora in high potential areas. Annual yields for fuelwood ranging from 5 to 8 cubic metres per hectare of agroforestry have been estimated. The rotation period can range from 2 to 5 years, perhaps including coppicing or pollarding (selective branch cutting). Typical values of 5.5 cubic metres (or about 4 tonnes) per hectare and three year rotations have been assumed for the present analysis on high potential areas and 3.5 m^3 (2.5 tonnes) per hectare on medium potential areas. The net impact on food production could be positive. By interplanting, the effects of shading could both dwarf some crops (e.g. of maize) and increase growth on others. Moreover, additional soil nutrients and soil retention can result. Leguminous or other nitrogen-fixing species such as Leucaena spp or Alnus spp can also provide nitrogen to the soil.

It should be noted that present production is approximately 1 tonne per hectare and that a fourfold increase will only be possible if a concentrated effort is undertaken. Of vital importance will be the development of a training and extension programme in agroforestry. Of equal necessity will be sufficient supplies of material, particularly seeds, and the development of high yielding tree species. The development of woodstick schemes has unfortunately been given very little attention, despite the fact that woodsticks, as such, form the most common type of fuel used on the farms.

The species selection and characteristics for agroforestry on low potential lands will be somewhat different, with generally longer rotation periods and lower yields. In addition, on both high and low potential lands, careful planning will entail selection of species appropriate to various altitudes. The details of agroforestry species selections and characteristics are presented in the technical volume on forestry opportunities, along with discussion of implementation approaches.

All agricultural land (about 7.8 million hectares) can be viewed as potential land for agroforestry projects by the year 2000. Since rotation times are short, production can be expected rather early for these schemes. In the late 1980's, annual yields of about 6 million tonnes could be achieved, followed by about 14 million tonnes in the early 1990's and increasing to about 22 million tonnes in the mid 1990's. By the end of the century a maximum of about 28 million tonnes per year of sustained yields could potentially be realized. This could supply about 39 million cubic metres of wood to rural households. In the year 2000, rural households are expected to require about 18 million tonnes of fuelwood, (out of a total national wood demand of 49.74 million tonnes) (i.e. close to 1 cubic metre per capita). Thus, if fully achieved, such an ambitious agroforestry target could result in meeting the rural household fuelwood demand by the end of the century and still provide wood for other activities. Thus farms may become exporters of fuel to towns and industry, and this could be a means of supplementing rural income. Therefore, there should be considerable incentive to promote agroforestry.

Replanted Forests

A ·major opportunity for wood resource enhancement with the potential for an early impact is associated with the clear felling and replanting of portions of existing natural forests with species whose characteristics are favourable for a high productivity fuelwood supply base. An additional feature of such a scheme would be that the forest resources could be managed satisfactorily, providing a high sustained yield through a rotation cycle of cutting and replanting segments of such a forest. Management could ensure a proper relationship between cutting, replanting, thinning, and the distribution of age cohorts within the forest. On the other hand, special attention might be required to maintain conditions appropriate to wildlife habitat requirements. The initial clear felling and replanting process, would, of course, be disruptive and here, too, steps to minimize such disruption could be taken.

The principal species identified for schemes in Kenya are eucalyptus and wattle (Eucalyptus spp and Acacia mearnsii). In addition to their favourable characteristics there is already some Kenyan experience with these species. It is estimated that a 10 year rotation cycle in high potential lands would be appropriate. Thus tracts of land planted in an initial year would be harvested and regenerated at the end of the tenth year of growth. Tracts planted in the second year would be harvested in the eleventh, and so on. On a given tract of land stocks are expected to grow to about 230 tonnes per hectare by the end of the tenth year. Thus once a steady state is achieved, i.e. tracts of land in each age group (first year, second year, etc.), a sustained yield of about 23 tonnes per hectare can be expected, while standing stocks will be in the neighbourhood of 165 tonnes per hectare.

Despite the rather long waiting period between the start-up of such a replanting programme and the first year of clear felling (e.g. 1985 and 1995 respectively), two aspects of this scheme allow for earlier impacts on the wood resource base. First, the clear felling of natural forest biomass can serve as a source of wood fuel from the inception of the replanting process. Typically, for every hectare cleared for replanting 50 to 100 tonnes of woody biomass will become available to service demand. Second, if additional early impact is desired, thinning during the course of the rotation cycle can be practiced. For example, thinning in the seventh year of growth can provide about 36 tonnes per hectare, with total stocks then growing to 179 tonnes per hectare by the end of the tenth year. With clear felling in the tenth year, average sustained yields in a steady state situation would be about 21.5 tonnes per hectare. While this is lower than the no-thinning practice it has the advantage of earlier impact. It is possible to increase thinning further to two or three times during the ten-year period, especially in the early years when the need for wood is particularly urgent, and shift to a full ten-year rotation for sustained production when crisis conditions have been overcome.

It is estimated that a maximum of 400 thousand hectares of natural forest conversion to eucalyptus, wattle or comparable species could be achieved by the year 2000. Under such maximum effort level, the wood resources derived from the clearing process alone would be in the neighbourhood of 1 million tonnes per year in the late 1980's and nearly 3 million tonnes per year during the 1990's. (This assumes for example, that 12 thousand hectares per year are planted between 1985 and 1989 and 34 thousand hectares per year are planted between 1990 and 1999).

The contribution from thinning (36 tonnes per hectare in the seventh year) would be about 0.4 million tonnes per year during the early 1990's and more than 1 million tonnes per year in the last half of the 1990's. Finally, harvesting mature trees would contribute more than 2 million tonnes per year beginning in the mid 1990's and about 6 million tonnes per year at the end of the century. Total annual supplies would increase from about 1 million tonnes in the late 1980's, to more than 3 million tonnes in the early 1990's, to an average of about 6 million tonnes in the mid to late 1990's. Beginning in the year 2000, when replanting has been completed, annual production would be about 8.6 million tonnes per year.

The systematic production of wood resources by clearing for replanting in the late 1980's provides an early opportunity for the introduction of more efficient charcoal producing kilns which would require economies of scale that could be satisfied by such a forestry operation. Thus, if only one-fifth of the wood supplied from clearing by 1990 were converted to charcoal by such more efficient means, roughly 20 per cent of charcoal demand in Kenya in 1990 would be met from charcoal produced in the new centralized kilns.

Periurban Plantation

Periurban plantations (i.e., urban greenbelts) have the advantage of being located near centres of urban population. Thus, problems associated with the logistics and cost of transport (including petrol costs) can be minimized. Under managed conditions, using species such as eucalyptus, wattle, prosopis, and leucaena, these schemes would have wood production characteristics comparable to those of replanted forests.

Periurban plantations would require the rededication of lands surrounding towns and cities from current usage patterns to wood production. Thus, the landtypes described earier as areas for urban expansion in each province would be the principal candidates of these projects. Since these are generally uncultivated agricultural lands and rangeland, this poses no major immediate threat to food or export crop production. However, in the future, should the desire arise to expand food and export cropping beyond the levels targeted in this study, there could be competition between food and fuel production. Some of the species mentioned above produce food and fodder as well as wood.

Since the areas available for periurban plantations will come from medium as well as low potential lands, two broad sets of production characteristics must be assumed. For high potential land the characteristics given for replanted forest, averaging 21.5 million tonnes per hectare yield on a sustained basis can be expected, under 10 year rotation with thinning. For medium potential land a 15-year rotation is assumed, employing thinning in the 10th year to obtain earlier impacts. With 32 tonnes per hectare in the year of thinning and 128 tonnes per hectare at the end of the rotation cycle, an average yield of 10.7 tonnes per hectare would be achieved once a steady state has been reached. These values have been assumed in this study. If thinning were abandoned beyond the early years, when its contribution might be necessary, an average sustained yield of 11.2 tonnes per hectare, and average stocks of about 85 tonnes per hectare, would be reached.

It is estimated that a maximum of about 200 thousand hectares of periurban plantation is feasible by the year 2000. However, except for early thinning and some sustained yields from tracts planted in the late 1980's, this scheme will not have a large impact on wood supplies until the end of the century. Thereafter, average sustained production of about 4 million tonnes would result at maximum levels. Thus, such a programme would serve three purposes for energy:

(a) to provide a small source of wood supplies,

(b) to help replenish standing stocks in the 1990's, and

(c) to produce a significant component of wood resource base for the early part of the 21st century.

While proximity to urban areas reduces diseconomies associated with transport, woodfuel demand in cities is dominated by charcoal requirements. Thus deriving charcoal from the wood resources from these schemes, using new more efficient kilns, might be appropriate. On the other hand, the need to reduce transport costs for forest supplies of woodfuel (e.g. from replanted forests), suggests that efficient production of charcoal might best be associated with forest supplies of wood. This may be especially true since agroforestry schemes could provide a large portion of rural energy requirements by the end of the century if an ambitious programme is undertaken. Thus periurban plantations and forest plantations might best be oriented towards charcoal production.

Industrial Forests

Agricultural land that is not used for growing crops can be dedicated to fuelwood production to service the requirements of large industrial consumers. The sugar, tea, coffee, and tobacco industries, especially, use substantial amounts of wood for their processing requirements. About 1.1 million tonnes annually are consumed by these four industries alone. By the year 2000 this demand could grow to 3.3 million tonnes. Industrial forests, then, could provide a steady supply of fuelwood to these industries, generally at or near the point of consumption. These forests could be plantations of species selected for their wood production characteristics on an ecozone or site-specific basis. Eucalyptus and wattle have been identified as having favourable characteristics.

The estimated potential for industrial forest plantations in Kenya is 50 thousand hectares. At annual yields of 21.5 tonnes per hectare the fuelwood supply from these schemes would reach 1.1 million tonnes once they are in full production. Currently, about 0.5 million tonnes are supplied from all "existing woodlots" (see Section 4). This can be compared with the forecasts of requirements for the industries discussed above. If phased in gradually, however, the additional yields in the 1990's would be 0.6 million tonnes beyond current levels.

Natural Forest Management

An opportunity exists for expanding the wood resource base
in Kenya by introducing management practices for existing natural
forests. This approach may be particularly attractive in that it
uses an already existing resource base and techniques that are
well understood.

Natural forests near centres of population can be managed
and thinned for fuelwood to help meet the requirements of the
local population. It is estimated that, once management is fully
effective, offtake as annual yield of woody biomass can be
approximately doubled. Since, at present, natural forests contain
a non-optimal mix of age classes, management can serve to bring
the forests to a more balanced condition. It could also help to
provide wood resources in an orderly and equitable manner.

All the remaining natural forest areas of about 850 thousand
hectares are potentially available for improved management.
Average existing yields in Kenyan natural forests are estimated
at about 2.75 tonnes per hectare annually, that is a total of
about 2.34 million tonnes. Moreover, only a small fraction of
this woody biomass (between 10 per cent and 20 per cent) is
accessible to the local population because of technology, labour,
and distance constraints. Under managed conditions, annual yields
could reach 3.7 million tonnes by the year 2000 and 4.7 million
tonnes on a sustained basis. Accessibility constraints could also
be minimized and most of this yield could be harvested for
distribution.

Even in remote forest areas the wood resources could be
transported as charcoal or wood (e.g. pelletized) to centres of
population. One intriguing possibility worth exploring is the use
of producer gas-driven trucks to haul wood directly. The producer
gas could be generated on site with about 1.5 M³ roundwood
substituting for 200 litres of diesel/petrol in conventional
lorries. The attractive benefits of such a scheme (avoided costs
for transport fuel, charcoal production, and/or pelletization)
suggest that further consideration be given to its feasibility.

Of course, these natural forest resources are not
distributed evenly throughout the country. For example, in
Nyanza, which is densely populated with substantial woodfuel
requirements, very little natural forest exists. A more complete
description of the prospects for introducing management
techniques into the various forests in Kenya is provided in the
technical volume.

Summary

A comprehensive wood resource enhancement programme, which
embodies the approaches and proposals discussed above, would have
to be elaborated in much greater detail once its broad contours

and direction have been identified as promising. Here we have evaluated the prospects and potential impacts of the major elements of such a programme, to serve as the first step in the process of refinement and selection for concrete policy development. Table 6.1, presents a summary of the characteristics and potentials for the schemes that have been discussed.

In addition to the implementation of general principles of forest management, particular attention should be given to the development of optimal fuelwood production systems which are linked to end-use demand. For example, wood stoves require certain wood diameter and length, as does a producer gas unit. But even for an open three stone fire, it is important to know approximately what the optimal diameter of the woodsticks should be, given the kind of food to be cooked.

This type of information will allow for the development of an optimal rotation period, and should also influence the optimality of fuelwood use itself.

Management and Extension

All the options mentioned above are dependent on good extension services and management. Without making adequate provision for teaching agroforestry techniques, short rotation and natural forest management and the growing of multipurpose trees, at all levels of training, then the various options have little chance of success. Therefore, worker training, college and university courses must be increased in scope, and sufficient places must be made available to fulfil the plans.

Increase Conversion Efficiency

There are two approaches to closing the gap between wood demand and wood supply. Kenyan energy policy must consider, in addition to supply enhancement programmes discussed above, opportunities for managing the growth in wood demand. This section reviews the feasibility of decreasing pressure on wood resources by improving the efficiency of wood stoves, charcoal jiko, and kilns used for producing charcoal from wood. No decrease in human amenity is posited here; rather we seek ways in which the energy input required to provide a given level of end-use service can be decreased.

Charcoal and woodburning stoves, including open fires, dominate energy end-use technologies in Kenya. Their efficiencies are considerably low and, therefore, considerable saving of energy could occur if a suitable stove design project was implemented. Recent experimental work has yielded some observations on stove design for fuel efficiency.

Table 6.1

WOOD RESOURCE POLICY POTENTIALS

tegy	Potential Area 1990 2000 (1000 Ha.)		Average Yield (Tonnes/Ha.)	Maximum Potential Yields (Million Tonnes Per Year)	Characteristics	Comments
Agroforestry High potential Medium & Low Potential	450 50	1200 300	4.0 4.0	4.8 1.2	High Potential-Principal species: Mimosa scabrella, Calliandra calothyrsus, Alnus nepalensis, Grevillea robusta, Leucaena leucocephala. Rotation 2-5 yrs. Average of about 12 tonnes per hectare at end of 3yr. rotation. Medium and Low Potential- Principal species:Cassia siamea, Acacia saligna, Prosopis sp. Rotation 3-5 yrs. Average of about 12 tonnes per hectare at end of 4 year rotation.	Primarily for rural fuelwood. There are about 7 million hectares of High Potential land and .8 million hectares of Medium Potential Agricultural land in Kenya. Currently about 3 million hectares of cultivated land expected to increase to about 4.6 million by the end of the century.
Replanted Forest High potential	60	400	21.5	8.6	Principal species: Eucalyptus spp, Acacia mearnsii. Thinning 7th year yields 36 tonnes per hectare. Yield in 10th year of 179 tonnes per hectare.	Portions of about 1.2 million hectares of natural forest cleared and replanted. Initial clearing produces about 100 tonnes per hectare.
Periurban Plantation High potential	35	190	21.5	4.1	Principal species: Eucalyptus spp and Acacia mearnsii Prosopis spp Leucaena leucocephala. High Potential: Thinning 7th year yields 36 tonnes per hectare; Yield in 10th yr. 179 tonnes. Medium and Low Potential: Thinning 10th year yields 32 tonnes per hectare; Yield in 15th year 128 tonnes per hectare.	100,000 ha around Nairobi plus 100,000 ha around other urban centres. Providing charcoal and wood primarily to the urban areas.
Managed Nearby Forests All Types	100	300	2.7 - 7.1	1.8 avg.	Using native varieties yields can double with management and thinning. Precise figures are different for each forest area, province.	Can provide charcoal and wood primarily to highly populated areas without major transport requirements.
Management of More Remote Forests All Types	200	200	2.7 - 7.1	1.2 avg.	Same as above.	Requires transport of wood or charcoal to markets. May reduce pelletization of wood or use of producer gas to provide economies in transport over longer distances.
Industrial Plantations High Potential	15	50	21.5	1.1	Principal Species: Eucalyptus spp and Acacia mearnsii. Thinning 7th year yields 36 tonnes per hectare. Yield in 10th year 179 tonnes per hectare.	Carried out by private sectors, primarily for crop drying and processing.
	9.15	2,650	-	22.9		

Power output should be variable over a wide range to match the varying demand of different cooking processes. High power outputs can be effectively absorbed in boiling but are wasteful for simmering.

Heat retention in high mass stoves may enhance the efficiency of prolonged cooking processes. However, low mass stoves heat more rapidly than high mass and tend to be considerably more efficient for short duration use.

The value of heat retention for space heating depends upon the relative usefulness of radiant and connective heat. High mass stoves can not be moved to suit heating demands in varying locations.

Enclosed fires may not be as well managed as fires which can be seen. Where stoves are designed with small fireboxes requiring small pieces of fuel which may be difficult to prepare, larger pieces are often used with the fire door left open. This may destroy the relative efficiency of the design. Leaving a door open for lighting purposes may have similar consequences.

Properly designed chimneys are critical to the performance of enclosed stoves. The chimney must be sufficient to remove waste gases but not so great as to induce over-rapid exhaust. A chimney that is too small will reduce combustion efficiency and a chimney that is too tall will reduce heat transfer, often to a level beneath that of an open fire.

Air inlet valves allow matching of the power output of enclosed fires to demand.

Grates improve primary air mixing and greatly enhance the efficiencies of both open and closed fires.

Proper balancing of primary and secondary airflows can ensure complete combustion without the introduction of unnecessary cold air.

Emplacement of pots in, rather than above, the hot gas stream dramatically increases heat transfer into the pot and simultaneously reduces heat loss. Thin tops, on enclosed stoves, are far better in this regard than thick tops.

Fire size should be matched to the pot as should the height of the pot fire. Both dimensions are, ideally, about one half the diameter of the pot.

The gas path should be designed to achieve high velocities at the surface, low velocities elsewhere.

Severally, or together, these technical transformations would easily allow a country-wide 10 per cent increase in stove efficiency saving 0.7 million cubic metres in charcoal production and 1 million cubic metres in stove fuel. In monetary terms, this would mean yearly household savings of Kshs 60 million on charcoal purchase and the equivalent of Kshs 100 million on fuelwood. A little investment could save a lot.

There are three important theoretical issues to be addressed in any stove programme, namely:-

(1) the design principles,

(2) the method of production, and

(3) the problem of diffusion.

The design of technology, particularly household technology, depends on an understanding of the interrelated systems of use, production and exchange. Without a proper matching of all these systems, designs will fail in application and the meaningful criterion for development - self-generating diffusion - will not be met. The problems of stove design for traditional energies pose two particular problems. Firstly, a technology frequently uses several different forms of energy. Modern technology designs are energy-source specific (e.g. an electric kettle, a gas cooker) whereas traditional designs are geared to multiple energy sources. It is difficult to design efficient stoves to accommodate all possible energy sources. Secondly, the technologies frequently service multiple end-uses. At the present moment, there are as many improved cooking stoves as there are cook stove technologists. Fuel efficiency is frequently the principal interest of the (usually male) designer but, for efficient stoves to diffuse, the diverse end-use reqirements of the user, usually female, must be satisfied. In particular, women may be more interested in saving cooking time even at the expense of collecting more wood: this is especially true if wood scarcity is not the womens' perception of the problem.

Recent stove design practices tend to focus only on one end-use - cooking - but traditional open fires have several end-uses including:

Rapid Boiling
Lighting
Space Heating
Maintenance of Thatch
Reducing Insect Populations

Preserving and Flavoring Food
Providing a Social Focus.

Efforts that essentially seek to improve the efficiency of
simmering (cooking) do so at the expense of other end-uses. Of
necessity, people require a multiplicity of end-use devices and
fuels which increase the real cost, in real and monetary terms,
of energy procurement. Stove design should be as concerned with
the understanding of social efficiency as with physical
efficiency.

Another important theoretical issue to address is the method
of stove production. Stoves are frequently seen as an ideal
opportunity for an "Appropriate Technology". Appropriate
Technology approaches, however, have certain characteristics
which, especially with reference to improved stove programmes,
are seemingly contradictory. In global terms, these
characteristics include:

(1) that they are a means whereby, if massively consumed,
    roughly 40 per cent of the world's population could be
    freed from a level of drudgery,

(2) that they will make more effective use of resources on
    an "As-Is" - "Where-Is" basis, and

(3) that the technologies are environmentally benign.

The second characteristic suggests that the technologies
will be locally produced and primarily small in scale ("Small is
Beautiful"). The first characteristic suggests that a large
number of small units be made. The conventional, and easiest, way
to make a large number of small units is mass production but this
contradicts the first, and frequently the third characteristic.
Stove production, in Kenya, faces the same contradictions. In
order to produce the largest number of efficient stoves, in the
shortest possible time, should multinationals be encouraged to
manufacture efficient stoves? Alternatively, should the artisans,
in the informal sector, be encouraged to improve their designs?
Multinationals will clearly establish monopoly conditions that
will preclude competition from the informal sector but,
simultaneously, will use effective marketing channels. The
informal sector, however, creates urban employment and recycles
resources effectively. The resolution of this conflict is clearly
a political issue.

In the Kenyan context, the debate about which production
systems should be used is ongoing. It is necessary, however, to
establish an effective stove centre to design and test stoves, as
well as cooking utensils. Such a centre could also promote the
use of more efficent stoves and train artisans especially in the
building of permanent stoves in houses. Most importantly, such a

centre would establish standards for stove efficiency and production so that the creativity of designers could be channelled, and monitored, to meet national needs.

However, even with the successful design and production of improved stoves, a central problem occurs with effective diffusion of stoves. In the Kenyan context, successful diffusion of stoves will probably occur most rapidly in the urban rather than the rural areas. Charcoal stoves, jiko, are already purchased in the urban areas and several fuel - technology combinations are available for other enduses, particular lighting.

In rural areas, the demand from women is currently for stove technologies that save labour not fuel. To this end, it is worth considering the diffusion of technologies that would simultaneously save fuel and labour time for cooking such as flour mills. It is worth emphasising that the demand for labour saving stoves could actually produce a design that increased the use of fuelwood. This demand however, is a realistic demand, at the moment, which reflects the relative local abundance of fuelwood in the rural areas. The situation will change rapidly over the next generation.

Kilns

Charcoal is widely preferred to wood as a fuel in Kenya. It has almost twice the energy content per unit weight, is easily handled and burns cleanly and evenly in simple stoves.

Virtually all Kenyan charcoal is produced in earth kilns. The energy conversion efficiency of these kilns is estimated to be about 24 per cent at best. Some charcoal (about 10 thousand tonnes) is produced in masonry kilns at twice this efficiency. The predominance of earth kilns is because earth kilns can be built to convert individual trees at the sites where they are felled, and can convert long and large pieces diminishing the need for laborious carrying and cutting of wood. Since charcoal production from Kenyan forests is largely proscribed, almost all Kenyan charcoal is produced from isolated trees, scrub, and private woodlots. The high cost of off-road transport of green wood precludes employment of stationary kilns except where high forest density reduces transportation needs.

Portable metal kilns are intermediate in cost and efficiency between earth kilns and stationary masonry kilns. But while these kilns are theoretically quite portable, lack of access to trucks drastically limits their portability in practice. They are also expensive. It is doubtful that the limited improvements in efficiency which they provide could justify the expense of purchase and transport.

Enhancement of charcoal conversion efficiency is likely to come either from masonry kilns or improvement of the earthen

kilns. A number of suggestions for improvement of the earth kiln
have been made. They include preparation of dry and uniformly
sized wood for even burns, use of a layer of sheet steel between
the wood and earthen cover to prevent contamination of the
charcoal, and various alterations of the burn path by means of
chimneys and stacking procedures. These modifications might
improve earth kiln conversion efficiencies to 30 per cent in
energy terms. Although technically feasible, these proposals are
not likely to be widely accepted, for the occasional and
itinerant nature of rural charcoal production renders extension
efforts extremely difficult.

The best prospect of enhanced efficiency probably lies in
construction of masonry kilns in conjunction with dense
plantation-type wood cultivation. These can achieve efficiencies
of up to twice that of existing earthen kilns. Masonry kilns
could account for a substantial fraction of charcoal production
if concentrated plantation cultivation becomes a major source of
charcoal feedstock. However, more modest targets of 10 per cent
by 1990 and 50 per cent by 2000 have been adopted here. The use
of a more efficient kiln in the charcoal conversion process will
necessitate that charcoal be produced on an organized, more
centralized manner, which contrasts sharply to its current
methods of production. But this latter production will still be
slightly above current production levels by the year 2000, even
if more efficient stoves and kilns are introduced to the expected
degree. At present, up to 20 per cent of charcoal is in the form
of powder and fines, and even with brick kilns, powder will still
be produced. If powder and fines are briquetted, then the
conversion percentage could be increased. One of the tasks of
current technology development should be the production of an
acceptable charcoal briquette.

Fuel Switching

Some observers, noting the profound effect of the energy
losses entailed in charcoal production upon the net efficiency of
domestic jiko use, have called for the renunciation of charcoal.
They argue that, as the conversion of wood to charcoal is 35-40
per cent efficient in modern masonry kilns and only 24 per cent
efficient in the earth kilns that supply virtually all of Kenya's
charcoal, a charcoal jiko would have to be 1.25-2.0 times as
efficient as an alternative wood stove to achieve parity in net
efficiency (neglecting the savings in fuel transport costs).
Furthermore, they claim that wood stoves can be designed to
attain fully the efficiency of improved charcoal jiko, although
present designs operate at twice the efficiency of their chief
alternative, the open wood fire. Use of such improved wood stoves
would require less than one-half the fuelwood consumed by an
improved jiko. Thus, if adequate fuelwood can be made available

to the urban households which now burn charcoal and if these households can be persuaded to switch back to wood, the demand for wood resources might be much diminished.

This change will not be achieved easily. Urban Kenyans (most of whom have paraffin or electricity available for lighting) prefer charcoal to wood for several reasons other than its economy. However, standardization of woodsticks or the densifying/pelletization of wood will make the introduction of woodstoves easier. It is worth noting that, for a cook without access to free wood, the net cost of cooking with wood or charcoal was approximately even, from 1975-80. With the publication of new, government controlled, prices for charcoal, which were brought in to reduce urban demand for wood, the picture has changed drastically. Table 6.2 shows that wood has become significantly cheaper than charcoal in the urban area, increasing the demand for wood. Charcoal requires little preparation, starts easily, and burns evenly for a prolonged period without attention from the cook. Perhaps because it is convenient, and a purchased commodity, charcoal also bears some relative prestige value. Unfortunately, most highly-efficient wood stoves fail to satisfy the most important of these criteria, convenience. These stoves depend for their efficiency upon the use of very hot, small fires. Constricted by design, their fireplaces will accept and burn dry finely chopped wood only. The fires burn rapidly and must be replenished frequently, yet the doors of the fireplaces, properly closed in use, make observation of the fire difficult. If this problem cannot be obviated by improved design, it is highly improbable that a significant share of the charcoal-using population will shift to wood despite price changes. It is also possible to modify improved portable jiko to burn wood and this may be one solution to encourage further switching back to fuelwood.

Table 6.2

FUEL COSTS IN NAIROBI, KENYA (US $/GJ)

Fuelwood	1.18
Charcoal	2.91
Kerosene	8.31
LPG (Butane)	13.61
Electricity	21.97

Such a shift could be motivated by a substantial change in the relative price of the two fuels. At least one observer has noted conscious price-based substitution of paraffin for charcoal (reversed upon announcement of a rise in the controlled price of paraffin). However, the labour budget implications of the substitution of these two fuels are trivial: the price-substitution effect may be much smaller with respect to the charcoal-to-wood switch.

As discussed later, there is considerable potential for the substitution of producer gas for the liquid hydrocarbons, particularly in rural off-road and stationary applications. The magnitude of this substitution could be very much enhanced by support of the development of a local generator unit industry. Solar water heating could come to displace an important fraction of electricity consumed for this purpose. Restrictions on installation of new electric water heating capacity could be very effective in accelerating a transition which is already cost-effective in commercial construction.

Certainly Kenyans express a great eagerness to shift to more convenient high quality forms of energy, e.g. gas and electricity. However, in view of the much higher costs of these fuels, their distribution systems, the appliances in which they might be used, and their potential to exacerbate oil dependency, near term policy emphasis must focus on using traditional fuels more efficiently.

Biomass Applications

Solar energy is captured through photosynthesis in organic matter. This "biomass" can in principle provide a renewable source of indigenous energy. Indeed, biomass in the form of wood currently accounts for three-quarters of Kenya's energy budget. An attractive possibility is the thermochemical or biochemical conversion of indigenous biomass resources to more useful fuel forms, especially those which could substitute for petroleum products.

We review several technological options for Kenya in the subsections below. Given the triple long-term resource policy goal of avoiding woodfuel shortages, decreasing oil requirements, and increasing food production, it is essential that indirect impacts of biomass applications be considered critically. Oil substitute schemes using wood should not exacerbate fuelwood shortages; the systematic use of agricultural crops and residues should be consistent with the maintenance of soil fertility.

(a) Alcohol

International interest in technologies for deriving liquid fuels from agricultural products has increased in recent years as a direct consequence of oil price increases. There are numerous demonstrated pathways for converting vegatative raw material to various fuels (ethanol, methanol, acetone-butanol, etc.) by the process of microbiological conversion under anaerobic (or air-free) conditions, dry distillation techniques as well as by other means.

Special attention has focused on the production of ethanol (ethyl alcohol), a substance which has been produced for beverage use since ancient times. Ethanol is produced by fermentation of simple sugar (glucose, fructose), either directly or from sugar first derived from plant matter of more complex molecular structure. The attraction of ethanol is its potential as a substitute for gasoline fuel in automobiles. Methanol (also known as "wood alcohol") could in principle play a role as a wood-derived liquid fuel, but the combination of corrosion problems in existing engines, current wood shortages, and the fact that ethanol is now produced on a tested commercial scale in many countries, puts only ethanol on the near-term planning agenda.

Kenya is actively engaged in developing an ethanol-for-fuel industry. The Kenyan Government has taken the majority share in two molasses alcohol plants currently under construction, with a joint capacity of 120,000 litres per day, although one of these plants (Kisumu) is unlikely to come on line. A third plant, based on sugar cane, has been proposed and is under active consideration. If approved, this will add a further 150,000 litres per day by 1985. In addition to ethanol, the programme is designed to provide feedstocks for the plastics and beverage industries. The goal is to blend the ethanol with gasoline in a ratio eventually of 20/80, the highest ethanol proportion not requiring engine modification.

Sugarcane and sweet sorghum are the crops producing the highest alcohol yield as shown in Table 6.3.

Table 6.3

ALCOHOL YIELD OF SELECTED CROPS, UNITED

STATES AND BRAZIL 1977

Crop	Alcohol Yield per Hectare (litres)
Sugarcane (Brazil)	3,630
Sweet Sorghum (US)	3,554
Corn (US)	2,200
Cassava (Brazil)	2,137
Grain Sorghum (US)	1,362
Wheat (US)	773

Additionally, sugarcane provides its own energy source for the conversion process in the form of bagasse unlike the other crops mentioned as ethanol feedstock materials. In Kenya, where abundant and inexpensive indigenous energy resources are not available, it would be inadvisable to use crops other than sugar.

Molasses, the feedstock of the first two Kenyan ethanol units, is a byproduct of cane sugar production yielding 280 litres of ethanol per tonne. Ethanol production from molasses is only economical if annexed to a sugar factory. Moreover, there are large opportunity costs associated with ethanol production. First, molasses is a strong foreign-exchange earner and, only between 1977-79 when commodity prices were low, was it realistic to consider burning it as fuel. Second, there is strong demand for molasses in cattle and pig production. These opportunity costs have not been given sufficient analysis.

The viability of scaling up the current ethanol programme raises some serious questions concerning its economic justification given the increasing demands for high quality land for food and wood production. Review of the status of the two molasses-ethanol plants indicates some of the dilemmas.

The first factory - the Kenya Chemical and Food Project - was to produce citric acid, baker's yeast, and vinegar in addition to its primary output, ethanol. Costs have far exceeded the original estimate of $55 million. The local market for the by-products is small (e.g., Kenya imported 58 tons of vinegar in 1979 while the plant capacity will be 2000), while successful competition in the export market remains problematic. Ethanol will cost about U.S. $1.90 per litre or about twice the pump price of petrol. At the present moment, the consortium building the plant has collapsed. It is unlikely that the plant will ever produce ethanol.

The other molasses-ethanol plant, the Agro-Chemical and Food Corporation, has a better location and is attached to a sugar factory but faces similar problems in that the ethanol is about the market price of petroleum (U.S. 60 cents per litre) and there are limited markets for the byproducts. Moreover, these two plants could not only be in direct competition with each other for the fuel market but also for molasses. Current estimates suggest that molasses may have to be imported in order to fulfil the demand for both factories, should both produce. No matter what decision the Kenyan Government makes about the pricing policy of ethanol, it will lose some U.S. $8 million per annum or, if it were determined to write off the whole cost, U.S. $90 million.

It is important to remember that the three successful examples of ethanol production arise because of the specific political economy of the nations in question, namely: 1) The United States, where ethanol maintains the global price of corn and there is no national food shortage; 2) Brazil, where an ethanol programme has run parallel to the sugar industry for 50 years and there is no food shortage; 3) Zimbabwe, where an oil embargo forced alternative solutions and there is no food shortage. In Kenya, with a food and wood shortage, the opportunity cost of ethanol production is necessarily high. Given the questions and uncertainties about the role of an intensified alcohol programme in an integrated food/energy planning framework, we do not include efforts beyond those currently committed in the alternative policy scenario.

(b) Producer Gas

Producer gas may prove to be the most valuable biomass-derived fuel in Kenya. An efficient substitute for the liquid hydrocarbons in virtually all of their applications, including motor transport, process heating and electric generation, producer gas can fuel existing equipment from boilers to diesel engines, with only minor modifications and little additional training of operators. It can be generated when needed and where needed, in a simple, compact, and inexpensive apparatus and thus is free from the storage and distribution problems which plague the use of alcohol and biogas.

Producer gas technology is well-known, predating World War II, when it was widely used in oil-short Northern Europe (over 70,000 units were in use in Sweden alone). Although the technology fell into disuse with the post-war flood of inexpensive Middle Eastern oil, rising oil prices have prompted renewed interest in producer gas. Several large-scale industrial and agricultural processing plants have been installed recently in Europe and the U.S., and the Phillipines is pursuing an electrical generation programme based on extensive use of producer gas. Several manufacturers are offering, on the U.S. and European markets, small-scale gas generators fitted to internal combustion engines: Brazil and the Phillipines have also produced cheaper models. Economically competitive in European and U.S. markets, producer gas technology will be far more valuable to Kenya and other oil-short developing countries, where imported hydrocarbons have much higher relative factor prices.

Producer gas is a medium-energy combustible gas formed by the partial pyrolysis and high-temperature reduction of carbonaceous solid fuels, most commonly wood chips, charcoal, or crop residues. Its principal combustible components are carbon monoxide and hydrogen, although it contains some methane. The relative composition varies with feedstock and conditions of production. When made from dry wood it approximates 20 per cent CO, 15 per cent H_2, 3 per cent CH_4 as well as some 60 per cent non-combustible gases, e.g. N_2. Depending upon composition the energy content varies between 4.1-5.4 MJ/m^3.

In large-scale applications the gas may be produced and burned in continuous-flow process, with efficiency as high as 85-90 per cent in heating uses. Most installations, however, are relatively small batch-type generators.

These units may be constructed of masonry in stationary applications, but are usually fabricated of molded steel, with cast fittings and tuyere (tubes). Many models are small enough to be mounted on a truck, tractor or car. In use, air dry wood blocks, charcoal, or compressed crop residues are loaded through an airtight door into the hopper/reaction chamber. The bottom of the reaction chamber is constricted, lined, and equipped with several small tuyere through which a regulated flow of air may be introduced. A fire is lit in this constricted combustion zone. It quickly attains very high temperatures, 900-1500 ^{o}C. Exposure to these temperatures occasions a spectrum of temperature-dependent reactions in the fuel above; drying in the most distant upper region of the reaction chamber, distillation in the next closest region, and thermal decomposition in the region immediately above the combustion zone. The gaseous products of these reactions are drawn, as demanded, through the high temperature combustion zone, where they undergo further breakdown and reduction, then through simple particulate filters, a radiator, and are fed directly into the intake manifold of a spark ignition or diesel engine.

A spark ignition engine (a conventional gasoline engine) running on producer gas operates at about the same efficiency as on gasoline, using 1-2 kg dry wood per litre of former gasoline consumption, but produces only about 40-60 per cent of the power it has when run on gasoline. Ordinary modern engines with large valves and relatively high compression operate at the high end of this power range after a simple advance in timing. Oversized engines may be used in high-load applications or, as in the Phillipines, a gasoline cut-in can be fitted to boost power for intermittent heavy loads.

Diesel engines running on producer gas still require some diesel fuel, about 10 per cent of their former consumption. Diesels running on this mix operate at their former efficiency using 3-4 kg of dry wood and 0.1 litre of diesel instead of one litre of diesel in conventional operation, and produce 85-95 per cent of their former power output.

High-quality commercial generators fitted to engines are for sale by European firms at about double the cost of the engines alone ($1000-$10,000). Many good designs are quite simple, however, requiring no unusual materials or techniques. It seems quite possible that such generators could be fabricated in Kenya by existing metal shops at a cost not exceeding KSh 10,000-15,000. Costs and quality could be stabilized by local factory production.

The great attractiveness of producer gas technology lies in the fact that it can be fitted to the efficient, flexible and reliable gasoline and diesel power units. Kenya has already made a substantial investment in purchasing and developing a service infrastructure for these engines. Producer gas-fuelled internal-combustion engines can, in principle, provide the power for rural industry, agricultural processing, rural transport, and dispersed electrification.

(c) Biogas

Biogas, like producer gas, is a medium energy (24 MJ/M^3) combustible gas derived from organic materials. Composed of approximately 60 per cent methane and 40 per cent carbon dioxide, biogas lends itself to a variety of applications. It may be burnt for light or heat or used to fuel internal combustion engines.

Unlike producer gas, biogas is generated by a biological process, anaerobic bacterial decomposition of its organic feedstock. The rate limitations of this biological process seriously constrain its applications. Production of useful quantities of biogas requires a large volume permanent culture. Such systems produce continuously and are not easily regulated. Thus biogas cannot be produced on an as needed/where needed basis, but must be produced at fixed generation sites and stored. Since it is not generally economical to compress the medium energy gases, gas must be stored in large volume leak-proof containers and distributed through fixed piping. These considerations preclude mobile application and impose heavy costs on high demand, intermittent uses.

Nevertheless, biogas has one overwhelmingly attractive feature; its input materials are comparatively cheap if water is freely available. The most common feedstock for biogas digesters are wet manure and crop residue. (Wood, which has a high content of indigestible lignins is not a suitable feedstock). The fertilizing value of these materials is not reduced but enhanced by their passage through the digester. At the same time, the action of the methanogenetic bacteria destroys many pathogens and serves as an effective sewage treatment. This ability to generate a valuable gas while treating and improving the quality of manure has prompted interest in biogas throughout the world. A simple technology has evolved and more than 800,000 biogas digesters have been installed, mostly in China, Korea, and India. Although there is considerable enthusiasm for biogas in Kenya, fewer than 100 digesters have been installed to date. Most of these are a locally made version of the design described below. This system, generally known as the Indian design, consists of a digester tank equipped with a floating metal cover constructed to collect and store the evolved gas. The storage chamber is connected by a pipe to mantle lamps or other appliances. In use, a mixture of fresh manure or other material and water, is fed through a submerged funnel into one end of the digester tank. The addition of this fresh stock displaces digested slurry through an outlet at the other end. Passage from input to output takes several weeks. Other designs exist, particularly for large scale digesters. The most notable variant for small scale use is the Chinese design, which substitutes a pressure resistant masonry storage chamber for the expensive floating steel gas holder. This design requires other scarce commodities: cement and masonry skills.

Most discussion of biogas has focused on its potential value
to the rural household, where advocates propose that the gas
could provide light, cooking energy, and some motor power. There
is more hope than realism in this projection. A typical family
scale digester might have a volume of 1.5 cubic metres. A local
digester would cost about Ksh 3000. Under good conditions this
digester would convert the manure of two cows into .75 M^3 of gas
daily. This amount of gas is sufficient to provide five hours of
lighting (100 candlepower), one hour of cooking (six-inch
burner), or to fuel a one-horsepower stationary engine for one
half hour. Storage capacity is limited to less than two days'
production. Even when a system of this size is functioning well,
its usefulness will be quite limited. Yet household systems are
not likely to function well consistently.

Biogas generation is not as easy as the simplicity of its
equipment might suggest. The temperature and chemical sensitivity
of the methanogenetic bacteria require careful management.
Digesters must be fed daily with material of the proper
liquidity, pH, and carbon/nitrogen ratio. A change in feedstock
or some other biological shock may halt gas production for weeks.
Gas production rates are strongly dependent upon temperature,
virtually ceasing at temperatures below 50^0 C. Mechanical
problems such as sludge and scum build-up and corrosion-induced
gas leaks plague digesters. Two recent surveys in Kenya found
that as a result of these problems very few (<25 per cent) of the
installed systems were actually producing usable gas.

While family systems can be economical under optimal
conditions, capital, labour input, and management costs will
severely limit their use. In India, where conditions are far more
favourable, the state supported biogas programme has been heavily
criticized for subsidizing a technology too costly and labour
intensive for any but the wealthiest farmers. While this problem
could in principle be avoided by development of larger, village
scale biogas plants, taking advantage of the considerable
economies of scale, dispersed Kenyan settlement patterns will
rarely support such plants. Even the Chinese acknowledge that
their biogas systems are built primarily for sanitary reasons,
with gas production as a side benefit.

In the Kenyan context, biogas may prove valuable in ideal
sites such as large farms, coffee plantations, and institutions
such as rural schools. However, for the foreseeable future,
Kenyan householders will not likely find biogas plants
worthwhile, and biogas can be expected to contribute little to
the overall energy supply.

Oil Conservation Opportunities

The Base Case projections indicate that Kenya's oil
consumption is likely to increase dramatically over the next two

decades. In the absence of major development policy shifts, oil will be required to serve as the energy foundation for economic growth. Indeed, the average annual growth rate for end-use oil consumption was found to be 6.0 per cent, implying a net import burden in the year 2000 three times the 1980 level of 13.1 million barrels.

The immense difficulties that the associated increase in the oil import bill would raise for long term development have been stressed earlier. It is important to stress that even if the use of substantial quantities of alternative fuels were phased-in over time, oil problems would only moderate, not dissipate. Oil will be the fuel used for the marginal output in the modern economy (the extra electricity generated, boiler fired, or kilometre driven) and thus will be required for growth in that sector in the future.

The conservation of energy - here defined as reducing the input energy required to achieve a given output of goods and services - therefore can play a critical role in minimizing the foreign exchange penalty of economic growth. The potential for conservation of oil in the generation of electricity through the substitution of alternative fuels will be discussed below. In this section we shall review the conservation potential for oil and other commercial fuels in the transportation, industrial, commercial, and household sectors.

(a) Transportation

Increasing the efficiency of the vehicular fleet must be considered a priority in energy planning. The projected consumption of petroleum products for the transportation sector is recapitulated in Table 6.4. This sector's share of the oil requirements was over 55 per cent in 1980.

With respect to private vehicles, there are two broad areas where efficiency increases could be effected: (1) improved performance standards for new and existing vehicles and (2) improved patterns of traffic flow.

In regard to the first area, the existing stock of vehicles will be largely replaced during the time-frame of our investigation. Consideration could be given to the adoption of minimum efficiency targets for new vehicles entering the Kenyan fleet. The recent increases in import duty on car weight is a precedential mechanism for affecting the character of the fleet mix. Purchase patterns have shifted in response to that policy toward smaller engine displacements (approximately 20 per cent of sales are now less than 1600 cc, compared to 10 per cent before 1980). Additionally, efficiency could be improved through programmes designed to upgrade the frequency and quality of vehicle maintenance.

Table 6.4

TRANSPORTATION SECTOR PETROLEUM CONSUMPTION (PJ)

	1980	1985	1990	1995	2000
Vehicle/Private	16.62	23.68	30.73	41.06	51.39
Petrol	16.62	23.68	30.73	41.06	51.39
Vehicle/Public	13.11	17.73	22.36	29.71	37.07
Diesel	12.38	16.72	21.07	28.28	35.50
Petrol	0.73	1.01	1.29	1.43	1.57
Rail	2.52	3.46	4.40	6.09	7.77
Residual Oil	2.52	3.46	4.40	6.09	7.77
Air	11.89	16.28	20.68	28.60	36.52
Jet Fuel	11.89	16.28	20.68	28.60	36.52
Pipeline	0.05	0.05	0.05	0.05	0.05
Electricity	0.05	0.05	0.05	0.05	0.05
Steamships	1.18	1.63	2.07	2.86	3.65
Diesel	1.18	1.63	2.07	2.86	3.65
Total Transportation	45.38	62.84	80.29	108.37	136.46

The second broad area, improvements in traffic flow, could also improve fuel efficiency. Congestion in the morning rush hour, complicated by use of automobiles to drive children to school, could be reduced considerably if school buses were widely used; changes in lunch-hour habits might decrease the rush of workers who drive home for lunch. Some improvements in traffic flow through the use of one-way streets in Nairobi is already apparent, but traffic circles at most of the major entrances to the downtown area remain clogged at peak hours.

There is also a great near-term potential for reducing energy use in Kenyan buses and trucks through better maintenance and, in the long term, through purchase of more efficient vehicles. The recent improvement in energy performance by Kenya Bus Service is encouraging, but could be further improved.

Private buses and trucks appear to be more poorly maintained than those owned by large companies, a situation which invariably leads to greater energy use. Existing vehicles in the large companies could improve their fuel use efficiency by about 10-20 per cent, while those belonging to smaller companies could achieve even greater reductions.

The railroad shows interesting trends. If its energy consumption is examined over time, a dramatic drop in intensity is seen. Total consumption fell from over 6.01 PJ in 1977 to 2.52 PJ in 1980. During the 1977-79 period the number of passengers increased 16 per cent, passenger train-km increased 39 per cent, while freight tonnage dropped 8 per cent. It appears that overall an increase in service has accompanied a rapid decrease in energy use. This was caused by a rapid shift from heavy diesel and fuel oil to automobile diesel oil, which burns far more efficiently in locomotives, and by upgrading of the locomotive stock as well. Unfortunately, recalling the refinery output characteristics, the shift is from an abundant fuel to a scarce one, which aggravates the already unfavourable relationship between oil-product demand and refinery output in Kenya.

Jet fuel accounts for significant energy use, suggesting that conservation could also be significant. However, sales of this fuel are especially profitable for the country as a whole, since airlines tend to pay in foreign currency. On the other hand, more efficient use of jet fuel would tend to hold down air-travel costs, which would promote foreign tourism and increase Kenyan foreign earnings. One of the reasons for recent increases in fuel efficiency (on a per passenger-km basis) is the use of wide-bodied aircraft, already common in Kenyan air traffic. Substantial further progress in fuel conservation will require the availability of the next-generation fuel-efficient jet aircraft into the fleets serving Kenya. There is little direct leverage here for Kenyan energy policy.

(b) Industrial and Commercial Sectors

Fuel and electricity use can be improved in these sectors by retrofitting existing equipment and designing cost-effective conservation measures into existing stock. In buildings, improvements could be made in the thermal integrity of building shells and in the efficiencies of lighting and other mechanical systems. Industrial energy use would benefit from improvements in housekeeping measures (e.g., turning off unused equipment) and process modification (e.g., recapture of thermal energy).

In industrial installations, the prospects for the retrofit of existing equipment are promising. A few factories have already achieved substantial energy savings through such low cost upgrading as added pipe insulation, thermostat control of refrigeration, and more efficient use of motors. But the majority of firms have not systematically investigated or implemented least-cost conservation strategies nor have they taken advantage of even the easier methods for reducing energy costs. There is an important role for government here in promoting conservation through information and education campaigns, provision of assistance with energy audits, and training of personnel.

In the longer term, as new equipment replaces old, possibilities for improved energy use efficiency increase further. Comparison of energy-use practices in developed countries suggests that new factories and equipment in basic industry could be considerably less energy intensive than those in Kenya today. Of course, future equipment selection in Kenya is difficult to anticipate; the availability of technical expertise is an important constraining factor. Government conservation outreach programmes (or possibly financial incentives) could put energy efficiency planning higher on the agenda for industrial decision-makers.

In commercial and institutional buildings, there has also been little conservation effort to date. The potential here for cost-effective energy reductions appears substantial. End-uses of particular importance for policy targeting include air conditioning and ventilating systems in office buildings, hot water heaters in hotels (where hot water heating accounts for about 80 per cent of total fuel use), and in schools and hospitals (about 50 per cent). In particular, solar water heating instead of conventional fuel and electricity use would offer quick paybacks and deserves further promotion over the study time frame.

(c) Residential

Clearly the primary conservation imperative in the residential sector is the more efficient use of wood and charcoal. Conservation potential for commercial fuels is constrained. End-use conversion efficiencies for paraffin stoves is already at about 70 per cent a unit for electric stoves; design improvement potential is minimal. Solar hot water as a fuel substitute may have potential but to be economical the structure of electric prices would need revision (in particular by removal of the two-tier off-peak tariff). Given the relatively small level of fuel consumption (e.g., residential consumption of oil constitutes less than 10 per cent of total 1980 oil used in Kenya), the low technological potential for efficiency improvements, the uncertainties in solar costs, and the importance of focusing on biomass use in residences, reducing commercial fuel use in homes should not be given high priority in government policy and programme efforts.

One interesting possible way of enhancing the quality of life particularly for rural people is by introducing acetylene as a light source. Acetylene was used (in Europe) for illumination before town gas and electricity became common. It is made by the action of water on calcium carbide. This latter chemical is produced by passing electricity through carbon and lime. Cheap off peak electricity could be used to produce calcium carbide and this possibility should be investigated.

Conservation Policy Issues

In addition to the need for increased educational and training efforts on the conservation investment option, pricing and incentive policies may have an important role to play in Kenya. There has been much debate in industrialized countries about the relative impacts on energy supply and demand of government policies regarding energy subsidies, taxes, and price controls. In Kenya the main evidence of price distortions was the price controls on charcoal, kerosene and gasoline, which kept prices for the latter lower than in Europe until early 1981. It is well known that historically low gasoline prices in North America led to inefficient cars and more driving than in Europe. The importance of market international forces in promoting efficient allocation of resources should be recognized.

The Kenyan Government should consider a policy of taxing imported oil, so that price will more fully reflect all the social costs of importing oil. This policy would increase the incentives of private companies to invest in energy-saving techniques. It might be argued that taxing energy would hurt industry, but the opportunities for conservation are so great that the effect on production costs could be kept to a minimum by good energy management. A desirable and possibly essential adjunct to this policy would be government assistance to industry in raising the capital necessary for investments in improved energy efficiency. Since taxation of any resources in a developing country could retard development, to remedy this revenues collected should be returned quickly to the economy. For example, such revenues could be applied to a programme of energy-efficiency investments.

Fiscal or other policy incentives that reward conservation should be considered. In Sweden, government loans and grants to firms engaging in heat-saving investments have had significant impact. The grant or loan is denied if the project is either very profitable to the firm (greater than 25 per cent rate of return), or unprofitable to the society (less than 6 per cent return). Although this programme has helped Swedish industry, some critics argue that it has also allowed less energy-efficient firms to "profit" relative to more efficient firms by making use of government money, and they suggest that a tax on energy use would be a better incentive. In fact, tax and incentive policies can both be used effectively to stimulate energy conservation. It should be noted in the context of Kenya's industrial structure, that the prominent firms are frequently transnational corporations and any policy that seeks to link increased energy efficiency with profitability would probably enhance the dominance of foreign capital.

There are situations in which the market place is inefficient, and government policies may be appropriate to deal with these market failures. Such failures include: the short time horizons considered by consumers purchasing appliances, cars, or houses; the lack of interest shown by builders in the energy costs of installed equipment; the lack of incentive by owners of rental property to invest in energy-saving measures. There is probably a role for minimum efficiency standards for major appliances, compressors, air conditioning systems, and motors sold in Kenya. However, only such standards as would promise clear economic and energy benefits should be considered. New commercial building codes that encourage the use of passive solar cooling would also be beneficial.

At present, too few managers are equipped to make straightforward calculations on the payback of investments in conservation options. More engineers need to be aware of the similarity of their energy-management problems with those of other firms.

Wherever it costs society less to save a unit of energy than it does to deliver an extra unit of energy, programmes to accelerate conservation activities may have a role. The government needs to define the end-use conservation opportunities where the costs of saving energy are less than the costs of delivering energy at the margin and explore appropriate incentive programmes to speed progress in this area.

Decreasing Oil Consumption for Electrical Generation

One of the moderately promising opportunities for reducing oil demand in Kenya lies in the electricity sector, through the expansion of generation modes. Of the 13.1 million barrels of oil consumed in Kenya in 1980, 0.96 million went to electricity generation. This is only 7.4 per cent of demand, but the figures for the year 2000 reflect the decreasing importance of oil-fired generation, which could be unrealistic. In particular, the difficulties of obtaining and repaying capital on new generation plant could allow the emergence of an ad hoc policy that favoured the retention of oil fired generation especially for peak demand.

While an expansion of non-oil options in the secondary conversion of electricity is only of modest utility in reducing the current burdens of oil consumption in Kenya, the issue promises to become more critical with time. At the same time, this potential can be employed as a basis for substituting electricity use for oil consumption at the end-use level. But, as long as extra electricity demand is associated with extra oil-fired generation, electricity substitution at the end-use will not be a viable means to save energy. This is due to the inefficiencies of oil generation where net efficiencies may be 20-25 per cent compared to 70-80 per cent for best quality on-site boilers.

In the remainder of this section, we review the potential for decreasing projected oil requirements through the use of alternative supply options. Generically, the phase-in of technologies not heretofore used in Kenya raises basic issues. For instance, the application of state-of-the-art electricity generation technologies is likely to require substantial amounts of capital, a resource whose availability is likely to be as limited as that of oil. Moreover, the operation of relatively experimental technologies implies a major degree of uncertainty with regard to their future costs. Any estimates of future performance could be incorrect by a substantial margin. Further, data on plant operations from highly industrial economies might not be replicable in the Kenyan context as problems of climate and ecology (e.g., excessive siltation) and operations and maintenance (e.g., the absence of sufficient trained personnel), come to the fore.

(a) Imports

At present, under an agreement with the Uganda Electricity Board, Kenya is provided with a bulk supply of 30 MW per annum. The experience with Uganda supply is indicative of the dangers associated with this mode of provision. While, in principle, Kenya might tap into extensive regional hydroelectric resources in Uganda and Tanzania, the Sudan and Ethiopia, in practice, a reliance on trans-national sources would be risky. For instance, the supply from Uganda has been subject over the past ten years to numerous interruptions due to that country's political

- 148 -

instability. Such considerations suggest caution would be prudent in deciding whether Kenya should rely on additional interconnected Uganda power (e.g., the potential associated with the Nile Basin). Tanzania also offers the prospect of bulk power purchases, especially as the wet season occurs in parts of Tanzania about three months earlier than in Kenya, and such purchases could thus be used to compensate for reduced stream flow. It also possesses substantial potemtial at Stiegler's Gorge, at a distance 800 Km from both Mombasa and Nairobi. However, the advisability of cultivating a dependent relationship between Kenya and Tanzania is once again contingent on a political situation that cannot be controlled to the same degree as domestically generated supply.

Another potential source of interconnected power is the (Nile) Rapids section of Juba. However, the international boundaries are such that the transmission of electricity from Southern Sudan would of necessity pass through Uganda before reaching Kenya. Thus, the problem of extra-national control over Kenyan energy resources would be compounded.

It is generally accepted engineering practice that no single generating unit should constitute more than 10 to 12 per cent of the total capacity of any electrical grid, so as to assure system reliability against the failure of any single unit. For this reason, the current National Power Development Plan for Kenya advises against firm contracts for imported power exceeding ten per cent, accounting for the possibility of precipitous cutoffs as a consequence of political considerations. On this criterion, a total of about 100 MW in 1990 and perhaps 200 MW in 2000 of imported power may be reasonable planning goals. The main drawback - security of supply - has to be tempered by the realization that the alternative of additional oil imports for electric generation also cannot be considered reliable. Considerations of relative economics and system diversity would suggest, in the short term, increasing hydro imports.

(b) Nuclear

The major technical drawback to nuclear power in Kenya, much as in other developing countries, is the size of economical nuclear units relative to the system as a whole. Where this ratio exceeds 10-15 per cent, there is a danger of cascading system failure in the event of unit outage which causes the remaining generation equipment to become overloaded. At the present time, the smallest commercially available reactors are in the 400-500 MW range. Thus, given Kenya's prospective annual peak load over the coming two decades, which is in the neighbourhood of 300-1000 MW, the addition of a single nuclear unit would imbalance the system substantially.

However, a number of technical developments in the field of nuclear and electrical engineering are operating in the direction of somewhat greater feasibility. A conglomerate of major nuclear vendors has developed a 200 MW pressurized water reactor "prelicensed, standardized, prefabricated barge-mounted...for application to small electric systems". This system is targeted for initial operation in about seven years and would require a lead-time of only five years. This new technology, coupled with major advances in switching technology, could lead to a situation where forced outage in a nuclear facility need not lead to cascading system failure so long as the nuclear generator represents less than 20 per cent (as opposed to 10-15 per cent), of total system capacity.

From a technical standpoint, these advances would allow the use of nuclear generators for systems of roughly 1200 MW or more, i.e. systems somewhat larger than Kenya's. In the Kenyan context, however, given the presence of additional hydroelectric and geothermal resources coupled with the small size of the overall grid, it would be fair to assert that, over the planning horizon of this study, nuclear generation is not a practicable alternative.

Coal

The current energy supply-demand disequilibria for Kenya would be alleviated through a "carbon solution" if extensive coal, oil, or natural gas were discovered in great quantities within Kenya. Though exploration has proceeded since 1954, no significant discoveries have been made to date. Over three quarters of the country has been mapped geologically, and 30 per cent of the area is considered to have carbon potential, especially the sedimentary basins in the Eastern, Northeastern, and coastal areas. Some coal has been found in the course of drilling for oil and natural gas. However, supplies are not in sufficient quantity and the depth of the seams is too great for viable commercial production.

Nonetheless, coal remains for Kenya a potentially viable "bridging fuel" in combination with other programmes. World coal reserves (exploitable with present technologies and at current prices) are nearly five times larger than known oil reserves. Geological coal resources are many times more extensive. While coal is found in many places, 97 per cent of presently known coal deposits are concentrated in developed and centrally planned economies.

Though ongoing efforts exist, there has been little intensive coal exploration in developing countries and basic geological data are inadequate. In 1973, coal output in developing countries represented only 6.3 per cent of total world coal production. Some 50 developing countries have known coal

resources and about 30 of these produce coal. Among developing
countries, India accounts for more than half of coal production,
and Yugoslavia, the Republic of Korea and Turkey for much of the
rest.

There are a number of grounds for an optimistic prognosis
regarding expanded coal use in Kenya, though the precise use of
coal within the current primary and secondary demand structure is
not clearly understood. In particular, recent exploration for
coal in the Southern part of Africa, particularly Botswana and
Tanzania, is yielding favourable results. There are known
reserves of coal in Mozambique. The development of an adequate
regional transport infrastructure could allow utilization of
these resources in Kenya. Furthermore, the logistics of coal
export from Western Australia to East Africa is especially
favourable. Australia has been estimated to be in a position to
export a minimum of 160 million metric tonne coal equivalent per
annum. It is reasonable to assume that East Africa and Kenya are
likely customers for at least a fraction of this coal, especially
if adequate coal handling facilities are provided in the form of
receiving terminals, ship unloading capability, and adequate coal
transport infrastructure connecting the coast and the high
potential areas of Kenya.

The cost of imported coal, while probably remaining below
that of oil, is nonetheless expected to pose a significant
problem for a country such as Kenya which is subject to severe
foreign exchange constraints. Moreover, coal today is subject to
increased cost due to substitution effects emanating from rising
oil prices. However, the general abundance of coal reserves in
comparison with oil reserves, coupled with the enormous
dispersion of coal deposits over many countries, suggests that
cartelization of coal is unlikely in the medium run. Coal prices
will most likely continue to be decoupled from oil. Thus, coal
imports, while a significant drain on foreign exchange, may prove
substantially less onerous as compared to petroleum imports.

Other Supply Options

The principal renewable supply options of relevance to Kenya
are geothermal, windpower, small hydro, and solar.

(a) Geothermal

As we have seen, geothermal fluids have been discovered in a
number of areas in Kenya, though to date only the Olkaria field
is being developed commercially. Current plans call for the
immediate completion of two steam turbo generators at Olkaria
totalling 30 MW. However, in addition to these Base Case
additions, at least 144 MW of potential capacity has been

identified at this same site, though development of the additional potential will be limited by topographic factors. Further, 326 MW of geothermal potential within Kenya has been identified for sites other than Olkaria. The feasibility of these sites is contingent on more intensive exploration.

(b) Windmills

Windmills have long played a role in satisfying the dispersed low power demands of rural development. Installed in favourable sites they serve end-uses from grinding and pumping to electric generation. In Kenya, windmills have been used for unattended water-supply pumping for over 70 years.

There are two major classes of wind machines, drag mills, the familiar low speed high torque fan mills, and lift mills, the efficient high speed low torque propeller mills. Drag mills are used for mechanical applications such as pumping, while lift machines are generally used for electric generation. Power, for both types of mills, is proportional to the swept area of the rotor and the cube of the wind speed. Thus an 8 M diametre mill generates 4 times as much power as a 4 M machine and a doubling of wind velocity yields an 8 fold increase in power.

Seven manufacturers currently offer windmills for sale in Kenya. Most of their products are drag mills designed for pumping applications. They range from the imported Southern Cross, to the locally manufactured Kijito, to the locally fabricated PU500. Costs per kW of capacity vary from Ksh 6000 to Ksh 20,000.

The economic feasibility of windmills is contingent on a number of factors:

(1). Available wind. In general sites are considered poor for windmill installation unless their average windspeed is 5 m/s. Kenya's equatorial location does not fall within macro wind patterns, so her wind distribution is entirely the product of local land features. Information presently available suggests that average windspeed of 5 m/s may be found in the Northern Rift Valley, Northeastern Central provinces, and on the Northern Coast. Marginal winds of 3 m/s may be found in the Lake Basin.

(2) Load matching. Obviously, windmills must be carefully sized to perform the work expected under available wind conditions, especially its variability. The windspeed distribution is quite critical. Furthermore, if winds vary and the power is not used directly, it must be stored. Water may be stored in reservoirs and electricity in batteries, but storage of adequate quantities of either water or electricity can be expensive. Costs frequently equal or exceed the costs of the mills themselves.

(3) Reliability. The critical importance of assured supplies of wind system outputs, such as drinking water, imposes a high premium on reliability. Dependable windmills tend to be expensive but breakdown of less costly machines may be catastrophic.

(4) Service availability. When mills do break down field service must be available. Despite their apparent simplicity, windmills are subject to very high stresses. Field repairs often require a fairly sophisticated understanding of windmill engineering, available only in a specially trained repair force.

(5) Dedication. Windmills are stationary and are usually capable of performing only one type of work. In many Kenyan situations investment in a more adapatable and mobile power unit such as a small tractor will be preferable.

(6) Capital market. Reliable windmill installations typically cost 50-100 per cent more than alternative diesel engines. Fuel savings may not be sufficient to amortize the increased capital costs under plausible assumptions on efficiency, discount rate, and fuel cost inflation.

Windmill applications currently feasible are restricted to drinking and stock water pumping in windy sites where maintenance skills and capital are available. Development of inexpensive but reliable machines would extend the range of this application to the Lake Basin and Coastal regions and might make use of windmills for crop irrigation marginally feasible in these areas. As seen, however, wind cannot be expected to serve as a nationally significant source of power for Kenya in the foreseeable future.

(c) Small Hydro

Small hydro schemes play a less spectacular but important role in the rural development of many countries. A notable example is China, where over 88,000 small hydro installations have been built in the last 12 years. Small hydropower installations (microhydro, if less than 100 KW, minihydro if less than 1 MW) are particularly attractive to developing countries for several reasons:

(1) Site requirements are not rigorous. Small heads and low flows can provide useful power.

(2) Although installation costs per unit capacity are higher than for most other power sources, the extreme longevity and low operation and maintenance costs can yield low life cycle costs per unit output.

(3) Capacity can be installed in small increments as demand grows.

(4) A wide variety of wheels and turbines are available to serve various sites and uses. Many of these can be locally built.

(5) Environmental impacts are usually slight.

The power capacity of a hydro installation is directly proportional to the head and flow available. A site with a head of 12 metres and a flow of 1 metre³ per minute can yield 1 kw. Installation costs for mini hydro plants range from 4,000 to 14,000 Ksh/kw, depending on site conditions and type of installation. These costs are typically broken down 24-52 per cent for civil works (e.g., dams) 30-40 per cent for generating equipment, 10-30 per cent for transmission, 3-8 per cent for operating and maintenance. A large proportion of these costs are domestic.

The economics of mini hydro, like that of windmills, is highly dependent upon the proportion of capacity which is actually used. Where availability of power or demand fluctuations are inconsistent, plants will be much less economical. Although existing hydrologic surveys are not adequate for precise evaluation, it appears that the high seasonal variation of most Kenyan rivers seriously diminishes their value for mini hydro installations. High capital costs and the relative inflexibility of hydro plants in relation to the chief alternative, the diesel engine, will preclude investment in many hydro units except by large landholders and government agencies. While exploitation of the hydro resources of the Aberdares and the Northern Lake Victoria drainage could have considerable local importance, it will not likely prove significant on a national scale.

Other hydro technologies which may have some local value are hydrams and river current turbines, both useful for pumping small quantities of drinking water.

(d) Solar

The study's assessment of prospective electrical solar applications for Kenya in the National Power Development Plan was on the whole pessimistic. Whether in the form of photo-voltaic cells or heat engines, costs under current technologies were assessed as prohibitive. However, some direct (non-electrical) applications of solar power are potentially significant including applications for water heating and crop drying.

Conclusion

     Despite the detailed consideration of alternative renewable technologies the next twenty years of Kenyan energy demand will be met from oil and wood. In the following chapter we attempt to provide a policy scenario for Kenya in which attention is primarily focused on meeting internal demand by focusing on supply enhancement and demand mitigation strategies that particularly seek to reduce the problem of deforestation while maintaining food and fuel supplies.

CHAPTER 7. POLICY CASE SCENARIO

The Base Case projection of energy and resources, as we have seen in Chapters 3-5, is premised on a continuous evolution of current trends in demographic, economic, technological, and policy factors. At this point, we wish to relax the assumption of continuity in energy policy intervention and ask some basic questions. If unprecedented governmental initiatives were taken to navigate Kenya's energy future, what are the contours of an adequate policy? What is the time frame for action? Can wood shortages be avoided and oil dependency reduced?

The Policy Case is a scenario rather than a forecast. The "scenario" can be a very useful device in energy analysis. If chosen judiciously, it presents a possible energy future for consideration and deliberation. While the Base Case posits a future scene which does not differ radically from the present in policy terms, the Policy Case scenario, on the other hand, is an attempt to present a possible alternative scene differing by one significant change in the script. Here, it is assumed that the government develops and implements an integrated set of conservation and supply enhancement policies.

It is not the purpose of the analysis to assign a probability for realizing a Policy Scenario. The function of the scenario lies elsewhere: to present alternative pictures of the future for assessing the relative desirability of sets of actions. Should the Policy Scenario be viewed as the more socially attractive option, its role is to help focus attention toward its implementation. Which scenario actually evolves is to a degree dependent on policy decisions. The role of scenario analysis is to provide the policy formulation process with information on the feasibility and relative impacts of alternative policy directions and thereby to aid in effective social planning.

Ultimately, the viability of energy policy measures must be assessed on the criterion of cost-effectiveness as well as technical feasibility. The optimal package of measures will provide the greatest net benefits. The costs over time (e.g., equipment, infrastructure, operation and maintenance, and labour requirements) must be tested against cumulative benefits. The benefits in the instance of wood schemes are complex and do not lend themselves to neat and non-controversial formulations in mathematical economics. Included must be the avoided costs of rural environmental degradation, and of the sundry economic implications of massive future wood shortages. The treatment of the economic trade-offs of Policy Case measures are contained in the technical volumes. Suffice it to say here that where conventional cost-benefit analysis applies (e.g., oil conservation measures), these measures appear quite attractive, while wood related measures appear to be imperative if national economic and social development goals are to be achieved.

Fuelwood Planning Goals

As we have discussed earlier, the disaggregated approach to energy supply-demand analysis permits the identification of the specific end-uses, fuel requirements, and resources for which problems exist or which will likely emerge over time. Moreover, it provides a quantitative basis for formulating and evaluating the full range of policy options that can have positive impact on the supply-demand configuration. This is particularly important in the development context, where scarce economic and institutional resources, already burdened by arduous development objectives, must be allocated with care and efficiency. Thus in the myriad of loci within the national energy network it is important to identify those for which policies can have a relatively large and timely impact for the economic and institutional resources diverted to their realization. The sectors and end-uses selected and described earlier (Chapter 6) have this character.

Central to implementing the fuelwood goals is the establishment of the institutional framework. It has been mentioned previously that good management is the key to success, and training courses for workers, supervisors and managers must be established or expanded. These courses should not only cover all aspects of forestry and agro-forestry management but the utilisation side as well, namely stove and kiln practice and design. This entails expanding vocational college and university training plus strengthening monitoring organisations and establishing a stove testing and extension centre.

There should be close co-operation between interested government ministries and departments, also non government organisations should be included in the institutional framework. Only through a concerted effort by government and the people will the goals be fully realised.

Demand Side Targets - End-Use Efficiency Improvements

About three-quarters of the fuelwood demand and more than four-fifths of charcoal demand in Kenya goes to urban and rural households respectively. It has been shown that there is substantial room for improvement in the efficiency of the end-use conversion devices using wood and charcoal, specifically stoves and jiko. Thus, a policy embodying substantial efficiency improvements in these end-use conversions, would go a long way towards eliminating the large potential wood shortfall facing Kenya. These improvements include a shift to improved jiko and cooking stoves in urban and rural households respectively, and a shift from existing jiko to more efficient wood burning stoves in some urban households. In these policy projections, an optimistic view has been taken of diffusion. Such optimism is only defensible if there is a rapid move to mass production.

(a) Improved Jiko.

The traditional metal jiko is used for boiling, grilling, and radiant heating. Alternatives, such as clay jiko, can be produced which consume half the charcoal required by the metal ones. They also perform better as radiant storage heaters so that heat is radiated more evenly. Although more expensive than the metal jiko, the pay-back time for the improved jiko is about 1-3 months, making them an attractive option. The policy target taken here is based on the premise that the government will encourage a major effort to mass-produce the more efficient jiko at low cost and to disseminate them quickly and widely throughout Kenya. This in turn depends on ensuring the availability of suitable clay and pottery skills. In our Policy Case projection, we have assumed that essentially all jiko (95 per cent) in Kenya are of the new efficient type by 1990.

(b) Improved Transitional Wood Stoves.

Improved stoves can replace the three-stone and other wood burning open fires used for cooking, space-heating, and to a lesser extent for lighting). A simple type consists of two parallel or converging lines of brick which form the side 'cheeks' of the hearth. The back end may be bricked in, leaving the front end open for refuelling. This arrangement, used in other countries, can be fuelled by steadily pushing in the burning end of a tree branch of 10-15 cms diametre and is estimated to consume at most two-thirds of the wood used for a three-stone fire. However it cuts down the firelight and if used where no direct lighting source is employed, will generate a need for separate lighting, probably involving kerosene, or in the future, possibly kerosene/ethanol mixtures or acetylene lamps (households that can afford electric light would not normally use a wood fire for cooking). Such an arrangement could reduce wood requirements by about one-third.

The policy target adopted here assumes a fairly wide dissemination of new stoves and management techniques in the rural sector, reaching 40 per cent of households using wood by 2000. A somewhat higher penetration in urban households and the commercial sector is targeted, reaching 50 per cent of those using wood stoves by the year 2000.

(c) Enclosed Wood Stoves.

These stoves completely confine a fire. They can be made from grass - or fibre-reinforced clay sides with a chimney connection and a top-plate made from cast-iron or from mild steel sheet (e.g., old car panels). Since these stoves require the development of a craft skill to build them, and since they would be significantly dearer to install than a new-style jiko, their penetration is expected to be small and confined mainly to towns. They need at most about one-third of the wood used by a three-stone fire.

These stoves might be more easily installed in new households as they are built. An alternative would be modified portable jiko to burn wood. The policy target adopted here assumes that by the year 2000 about 20 per cent of all urban households that would otherwise use charcoal jiko would switch to these stoves given the appropriate policy initiatives.

It is most important to realize that all three of the end-use demand reducing measures described above (jiko, hearths, and stoves) will require a concentrated effort to mount a vigorous public information and demonstration programme involving steady pressure in the media and woodfuel centres throughout the country. A central stove testing and training centre should be established without delay. This would look into the design of all kinds of stoves and run courses for artisans or teachers, who would thus disseminate the knowledge throughout the country. Such a centre would also look into the design of pots and pans, briquetting techniques, firelighters, kiln design and material use. A training programme would be needed to teach operatives how to demonstrate and give advice on the use of these devices to the public.

(d) Kiln Efficiency Improvements

Another demand reducing policy that has been included in the Policy Case is the introduction of more efficient kilns for charcoal production. As discussed earlier, metal and masonry kilns exist that can produce about twice the charcoal obtainable from traditional earthen kilns; that is, about 6 cubic metres of wood per tonne of charcoal instead of 12 cubic metres per tonne. Special pyrolysis units, although more expensive, have even greater efficiencies (4.5 m^3 to 1 tonne). If the powder and fines are briquetted, the theoretical limit is 3.5 cubic metres of air-dry wood (15 per cent-moisture) for producing one tonne of charcoal (5 per cent moisture -content), but this can never be reached in practice as a good deal of the carbon is converted into volatile organic liquids and low valve gases. These can, however, be captured by the more advanced pyrolysis units.

It is clear from the costs and production characteristics of the newer kilns, discussed in Chapter 6, that scale economies would be needed in order that these kilns penetrate the charcoal production sector in a major way. Under current conditions and practices, production is generally dispersed and performed on a small scale, using wood resources from rangeland, savannah bush land, and some farms. Where wood resources are not sufficiently dense it would be inconvenient and costly either to haul wood to larger kilns over long distances or to transport the kilns by some means such as lorries. The magnitude of throughput requirements of the new kilns is much higher than traditional earthen kilns. It is clear, then, that the kiln strategy must be closely linked to the production of charcoal at the sites of new large scale wood production projects.

As a consequence of the above considerations, the kiln strategy, while logically a demand reduction option, is closely linked with wood resource enhancement (or supply) policy. Therefore, anticipating the targets and results of supply side policies, discussed below, we have estimated the supplies of wood resources deriving from the various wood production projects embodied in the Policy Case. From clear felling and thinning of trees in projects for replanting natural forests, more than one (1.3) million tonnes of wood per year will be available beginning in 1991 (about twice that in the late 1980's). Using new and improved kilns, this resource alone could provide about fifty per cent of all charcoal requirements in Kenya by 1990. If one included resources from management of natural forests as well, all of charcoal demand could be derived from production in the new kilns. We have made a more cautious assumption, however, regarding the early introduction of new kilns. Only ten per cent of charcoal production is assumed to occur in this way by 1990, as a result of policy initiatives. This is primarily because of the reorganisation of the charcoal production and distribution practices that would inevitably accompany such a shift in resource base and operating conditions. A similar estimate shows that by 2000 up to forty per cent of all charcoal requirements in Kenya could be met by new kilns using the sustained yields from replanted forests. Here again, natural forest resources could increase this to seventy per cent of charcoal requirements. And here, too, we have assumed a more modest target, fifty per cent penetration of new kilns by the year 2000.

Table 7.1 summarizes the Policy Case implementation targets and wood resource savings characteristics of each of the demand side policies, both at the end-use and at the intermediate conversion stages of the supply/demand process.

Supply Side Targets

A number of considerations informed the development of the wood resource targets embodied in the Policy Scenario. First the impacts of the demand side policy targets were examined. Through increasing wood conversion efficiencies both in end-uses and at kilns, an initial step in reducing the burden on existing supplies of wood resources will have been taken. While these measures will not entirely be in place prior to the projects we shall propose to enhance wood resources, it is nonetheless

Table 7.1

WOOD DEMAND POLICY CHARACTERISTICS AND IMPLEMENTATIONS

Strategy	Penetration 1990	2000	Wood Savings 1990	2000	(Million Tonnes)
End-Uses					
Improved Wood	5%	20%	.01	.10	Urban
Stoves	10%	40%	.68	3.70	Rural
Switch Charcoal	5%	5%	.37	.72	Char. Wood Saved
to Wood (urban)			-.05	-.11	Increased Fuelwood
Improved Jiko	95%	95%	3.69	7.16	Urban
	100%	100%	1.44	1.83	Rural
End-Use Subtotals			6.14	13.40	
Intermediate Conversions					
Improved Kiln	10%	50%	0.36	2.96	All
Totals			6.50	16.36	

Note: Charcoal consumption savings are calculated before kiln improvement effects, so that the totals represent the full savings between the Base and the Wood Policy cases.

essential to see how far the pressure on the existing resource base can be reduced through the introduction of efficent, cost-effective conversion technologies.

With the demand-reducing measures assumed in-place, regional wood shortfalls are of course decreased relative to Base Case levels. The next step is to compare these remaining shortfalls with the maximum potentials for the wood resource schemes discussed in the beginning of Chapter 6. Then specific regional shortages still remaining in the presence of the demand-side policies can be addressed by phasing in all or part of the resource policy potentials for each region. In so doing, one has the opportunity to test the potential for eliminating stock depletion - indeed for restoring the wood resource base - as well as eliminating wood supply shortages. The Policy Case targets developed here address both of these objectives. Nonetheless, it would be excessively optimistic to assume that the gap between wood supply and demand in Kenya, which otherwise threatens to grow rapidly over the next two decades, can be kept closed throughout this period. A more modest, yet quite ambitious, objective is established here. Given the financial, physical, institutional, and logistical constraints inherent in the implementation of an ambitious wood resource enhancement programme in Kenya, a goal of closing the gap between requirements and resources by the end of the century is set. At the same time, we shall see that the maintenance and restoration of the standing stock will have been approached so that the country would enter the 21st Century with a sustainable biomass resource base.

Table 7.2 presents the principal results of the demand side policies alone on a national basis and compares them to Base Case findings. One can observe that on a national basis the wood shortfall or gap has been reduced to 9.58 million tonnes by 1990 and 23.70 million tonnes by the year 2000. This can be compared with Base Case results of 10.58 and 32.61 million tonnes shortfall for these two years. Demand side targets thus have a very large impact by the end of the century but a modest impact in the near term. Demand policy also reduces cumulative stock depletion from about 20 per cent to 14 percent. It is important to remember that the percentage stock depletion picture understates the ecological impact on remaining trees since much of the stock will have been denuded, with much of the branch structure removed.

The results indicate that substantial additional effort is required on a national basis, beyond the demand side policy targets, if the growing wood shortage in Kenya is to be eliminated by the end of the century. The magnitude and timing of this remaining shortage has been examined on a regional basis as well to establish targets, less ambitious than before, for wood resource polices.

Table 7.2

DEMAND SIDE WOOD POLICY IMPACTS ON RESOURCE BASE IN KENYA
POLICY VERSUS BASE CASE - NATIONAL SUMMARY (MILLIONS OF TONNES)

| | 1990 | | 2000 | |
	Base Case	Policy Case	Base Case	Policy Case
Demand	32.37	26.23	49.74	36.34
Supplied	21.57	16.65	17.13	12.65
From Yields	8.06	8.24	4.97	5.75
From Stocks	13.51	8.42	12.16	6.89
Shortfall	10.80	9.58	32.61	23.70
Standing Stocks	829.36	842.51	674.40	714.96

Table 7.3

WOOD PROJECT POLICY CASE NATIONAL TARGET IMPLEMENTATIONS*

Strategy	Cumulative Areas 1990 2000 (1000 Hectares)		Actual Yield 2000	Ultimate** Sustainable Yields
			(Million Tonnes/Year)	
Agroforestry	983	2660	10.63	10.64
Replanted Forest	81	306	5.38	6.58
Periurban Plant	51	165	3.82	3.44
Managed Near Forest	116	260	.63	1.56
Managed Far Forest	180	180	.64	1.08
Industrial Plantation	14	39	.82	.84
Totals	1425	3610	21.92	24.14

*   See Table 6.1 for assumptions on wood scheme characteristics and potentials.

** Average annual yields from sustained harvesting of a uniform age, distribution of wood projects.

Table 7.4

WOOD RESOURCE POLICY TARGETS (1000 HECTARES)

Provinces		Replanted Forest	Manage Nearby Forest	Manage Remote Forest	Peri-Urban Plantation	Industrial Plantation	Agro-Forestry	Total Land Targeted	Total High and Medium Potential Land
Central/Nairobi	1990	19	34	5	25	6	74	495	1,387
	2000	100	70	5	105	15	200		
Coast	1990	6	6	5	1	-	60	190	1,421
	2000	15	15	5	5	-	150		
Eastern	1990	13	6	5	6	0	161	514	2,964
	2000	40	15	5	10	4	440		
North Eastern	1990	-	-	-	2	-	-	5	-
	2000	-	-	-	5	-	-		
Nyanza	1990	1	-	-	7	-	166	416	1,252
	2000	1	-	-	15	-	400		
Rift Valley	1990	40	56	165	7	6	402	1623	3,458
	2000	130	128	165	15	15	1170		
Western	1990	2	14	-	3	2	120	367	823
	2000	20	32	-	10	5	300		
Total	1990	81	116	180	51	14	983	3,610	11,300
	2000	306	260	180	165	39	2660		

Table 7.5

POLICY CASE WOOD RESOURCE SUPPLY-DEMAND RELATIONSHIP IN KENYA
(MILLIONS OF TONNES)

	1990		2000	
	Base Case	Policy Case	Base Case	Policy Case
Demand	32.37	26.23	49.74	36.35
Supplied	21.57	19.27	17.13	34.07
From Yields	8.06	12.91	4.97	29.74
From Stocks	13.51	6.35	12.16	4.33
Shortfall	10.80	6.96	32.61	2.28
Standing Stocks	829.36	839.45	674.40	799.92

Table 7.6

WOOD RESOURCES ON CULTIVATED LAND
POLICY CASE (MILLION TONNES)

| | Wood Resources on Cultivated Land | | | | |
	1980	1985	1990	1995	2000
Stocks (million tonnes)	32.51	27.13	25.67	25.35	24.55
Area (million hectares)	2.95	3.37	3.79	4.21	4.63
Stocks/Area (tonnes/hectare)	11.02	8.05	6.77	6.02	5.30
Per cent decrease of wood density		27	39	45	52

Table 7.7

POLICY CONTRIBUTIONS TO CLOSING THE GAP BETWEEN WOOD
REQUIREMENTS AND SUPPLIES

	Years 1990	2000
Base Case Gap	10.8	32.6
Demand Reduction Policies		
Improved Wood Stoves	.6	3.7
Improved Charcoal Stoves	5.5	9.7
Improved Charcoal Kilns	.3	2.9
Demand Total	6.4	16.3
Supply Enhancement Policies		
Agro-Forestry	3.86	10.63
Replanted Forests	0	5.38
Managed Forests	1.75	2.59
Peri-Urban Plantations	0	3.66
Industrial Fuel Plant	0	0.82
Increased Natural Yields	.77	1.51
Decreased Wood Stock Depletions	-2.00	4.91
Supply Total	2.6	27.1
Policy Case Gap	1.7	0.0

(All quantities are in millions of metric tonnes)

The characteristics and implementation targets for these resource enhancement schemes, included in the Policy Case are given below in Table 7.3. Region specific targets are presented in Table 7.4. Each province has its own specific problems with wood supply-demand balance. And in each province specific opportunities exist for addressing these problems. For example, while Nyanza does not have significant forest resource potential, the potential for agroforestry in its densely populated rural areas provides the basis for the relatively high agroforestry target in this province.

Long Term Impacts

The principal impacts of the combined wood demand and supply policy targets are summarized, on a national basis, in Table 7.5. As can be seen the expected national shortfall for the year 2000, reduced from 49.74 million tonnes to 36.34 million tonnes by demand policies (see Table 7.2), is almost eliminated by the addition of the resource policy targets given above (Table 7.3). By 1990 these reductions are not as dramatic. An expected Base Case shortfall of 10.80 million tonnes is reduced to 9.58 by demand policies (Table 7.2), and is further reduced to by supplementing these with the resource enhancement policies (Table 7.5). Thus, while the near term improvement is substantial (about 64 per cent of the expected 1990 gap is closed), the remaining shortfall during the middle part of the next two decades presents an additional challenge to energy/development policy formulation. We shall return to this in the final section of this chapter.

Other important results emerge from the Policy Case analysis. It can be seen from Table 7.5 that stock depletion is substantially reduced by the combination of demand and supply policies. Table 7.6 shows that wood stock density on cultivated lands which could otherwise face cumulative reduction of 74 per cent (Table 5.16) would decline by only 52 per cent in the Policy Case. More significantly, the process of stock restoration will be well under way by the end of the century.

A more detailed breakdown of the contributions of the various components of the Policy Case targets to reducing the potential wood shortfall in Kenya, is given in Table 7.7.

Here it should be noted that there are interactive and indirect effects of both demand and supply side policy implementations. In estimating the contributions of each policy component to reducing the wood resource requirements, the effects of the end-use improvements were calculated first by assuming no other changes in the system, then the effects of the intermediate conversion improvements were calculated, and finally the effects of the various wood supply projects. Thus, for example, the impacts of stove and jiko improvements were accounted first, then the kiln improvements affecting the remaining wood requirements for charcoal production. The impacts of the wood resource enhancement schemes include both the direct contributions of their sustained yields to the wood shortfall reduction, and their indirect impacts through diminished stock depletion and increased yields of naturally occurring resources in some provinces for fuelwood supply. A similar indirect effect on the natural wood supply occurs as a result of demand reduction.

Examination of province-specific results is also instructive. This shows that with the given targets embodied in the Policy Case two provinces, Nyanza and Western, would still face significant shortfalls by the year 2000 of 28 and 16 per cent of their respective demands respectively. These are the provinces that are now facing the most severe near term problems. Since it takes time to phase in the policy targets, and since the opportunities for some policies are limited in these provinces (e.g. forest resource enhancement in Nyanza), some further policy attention would be required if the gap in these provinces is to be closed by the end of the century. While it would be possible to consider increased implementation of the original policy targets (for example more agroforestry), we have chosen here to remain within the limits set earlier. Instead, noting the prospect for substantial resource enhancement in other provinces, Rift Valley in particular, the Policy Case assumes that the regional surpluses available in one or more of these provinces can be made available to Nyanza and Western provinces. This of course would require the transport of these resources in the form of fuelwood, charcoal and/or pelletized wood, depending upon the particular sectors for which they are destined.

Oil Reduction Targets and Impacts

In addition to building toward supply/demand balancing of wood resources, energy policy must also address the problem of controlling the growth of oil requirements. In Chapter 6, we have discussed the basic options to conserve or substitute for oil consumption. The most promising of these on the criteria of feasibility, reliability, and likely cost-effectiveness have been used to develop oil reduction goals for the Policy Case scenario.

Quantification of plausible reduction targets is of course inherently uncertain under the best of circumstances. Limitations on basic data on the way oil is used at the end-use - building thermal control, process practices, boiler efficiencies, vehicular efficiencies, and so on - compound the difficulties. Nevertheless, on the basis of the survey information available to date, estimates have been developed.

Some of the policy issues relevant to increasing the efficiency of the country's oil-using equipment have been discussed in Chapter 6. The detailed formulation of appropriate policy strategies - education and training, pricing and

incentives, standards and regulation - are beyond the scope of
this investigation. They would need to be established through a
process which would improve and systematize the existing data
bases, establish efficiency target goals, and be tailored to the
institutional constraints and opportunities for each economic
sector.

For illustrative purposes, however, we have developed some
preliminary targets for decreasing oil consumption from Base Case
levels. Based on our current estimate of consumption
characteristics at the end-use, the Policy Case targets presented
in Table 7.8 appear technically feasible, cost-effective, and
achievable through governmental energy policy. The basis for
these targets is discussed in Chapter 6 and the technical
volumes.

The resulting Policy Case forecast of sources and uses of
oil are displayed in Table 7.9 and contrasted with the
corresponding Base Case results. Several aspects are noteworthy.
First of all, the reduction in refined import requirements is
disproportionately greater than overall reductions amounting to
24.0 per cent and 26.0 per cent in 1990 and 2000, respectively.
This is due to the use of imported refined oil as a marginal
source. This means that in evaluations of conservation
investments from a social cost point of view, conservation costs
should be compared with projected costs of imported refined oil.
Or alternatively, if additional refinery capacity is created to
avoid importing the higher priced refined oil, the conservation
measures are a substitute for crude oil imports and the
additional refinery costs which would be required in the absence
of the measure.

The overall reduction in import requirements is 13 per cent
by the year 1990 and 18 per cent by 2000. The major impacts are
in the transportation, large industry, and electricity generation
sectors. Substitution for oil-fired generation holds great
promise, since again oil is the marginal fuel. Reduction of
demand through end-use efficiency improvements or development of
non-oil using capacity both directly displace oil. In the Policy
Case, the reduction of oil for generation is 54 per cent in 1990
and 41 per cent in 2000. The comparative information is presented
in Table 7.10. Of the overall reduction in oil generation of 667
GWh in 1990 and 1376 GWh in 2000, over 70 per cent is due to the
substitution of additional imports and new hydro and geothermal.
(The rest is a result of end-use efficiency improvements.)
Additionally, some 300 MW of oil-fired capacity expansion can be
avoided.

Table 7.8

POLICY CASE REDUCTION TARGETS

Sector	Target
Large Industry	Oil use reduction* of 20%, electricity use reduction* of 15% by 1990
Commercial/Institutional	All fuel use reduction* of 15% by year 1990
Transportation	Vehicular consumption reduction* of 10% by 1990 and 20% by 2000
Electricity Generation	Additional imported hydro** of 50 MW by 1990 and 100 MW by 2000

*   Relative to Base Case
** Beyond Base Case level of 30 MW

Table 7.9

OIL SOURCES AND USES POLICY VERSUS BASE CASE

	Base Case	1990 Policy Case	Reduction	Base Case	2000 Policy Case	Reduction
Sources (million barrels)						
Imported Crude	26.3	23.8	10	26.3	26.3	-
Imported Refined	4.2	2.8	33	24.1	15.1	37
Total Sources	30.5	26.6	13	50.4	41.4	18
Uses+ (million barrels)						
Large Industry	6.22	4.98	20	12.81	10.25	20
Transportation	12.84	11.99	7	21.82	18.99	13
Commercial	.28	.24	14	.52	.44	15
Elec. Generation	3.10	1.43	54	8.68	5.15	41
Other	3.86	3.86	-	5.77	5.77	-
Total	26.30	22.50	14	49.60	40.60	18

\+ Difference between sources and uses due to refinery loss and export of refined oil products.

Table 7.10

ELECTRICAL GENERATION POLICY VERSUS BASE CASE

		1990		2000	
		Base Case	Policy Case	Base Case	Policy Case
Oil Steam	(MW)	152	93	579	265
	(GWh)	667	0	2,537	1,161
Imported Hydro	(MW)	30	80	30	130
	(GWh)	237	631	237	1,025
Geothermal	(MW)	45	45	100	100
	(GWh)	118	114	263	263
Other	(MW)	622	600	872	872
	(GWh)	2,647	2,628	3,742	3,742
Total	(MW)	849	818	1,581	1,367
	(GWh)	3,669	3,372	6,779	6,190

CHAPTER 8   SUMMARY AND CONCLUSIONS:
            TOWARD A SUSTAINABLE ENERGY FUTURE

     This volume outlines the programmatic options in energy
planning that the Government of Kenya should consider. It is
based on the accumulated experience of four years work in Kenya
by staff of the Ministry of Energy and the Beijer Institute. This
volume outlined a strategy that placed much emphasis on
developing indigenous biomass sources for fuel supplies over the
next twenty years; this strategy is essential if Kenya wishes to
decrease energy dependence.
     The analysis summarised current consumption patterns in both
modern and traditional sectors, emphasising the critical role
that fuelwood plays in the energy economy. The analysis was based
on an energy accounting system, LEAP (LDC Energy Alternatives
Planning Model), which was specifically developed to encompass
the Kenyan energy system. It has since been expanded to other
Third World contexts. Included in the energy accounting system
was a detailed analysis of landuse which allowed consideration of
forestry as a competitive or non-competitive activity vis-a-vis
agricultural production in light of current landuse practices.
     The Base Case Scenario projected energy consumption under
the assumption that current development patterns, both in general
but especially in energy, will continue. The basecase
demonstrated clearly that, not only will there be a significant
increase in hydrocarbon utilisation, but that deforestation will
accelerate at an unprecedented pace a pattern that is not
sustainable. A variety of conservation and supply strategies were
examined which could potentially ease the current situation and
enhance indigenous energy production over the next 20 years.
     An integrated energy plan must be developed at this point in
Kenya's history if serious impending crises are to be avoided.
The dimensions of the twin problems of increasing wood shortages
and oil dependence, which can be expected in the absence of such
a plan (the Base Case projection), have been outlined in Chapter
5. Wood resource requirements will increase from 20.4 million
tonnes in 1980 to 49.7 million tonnes by 2000. Shortfalls will
reach 11 million tonnes by 1990 and 33 million tonnes by 2000.
Oil imports will almost triple by 2000 with the corresponding
pressure on foreign exchange earnings (oil costs at perhaps
fourteen times current export earnings) threatening to brake
modernization efforts.
     The massive shortfalls of wood supplies to meet household
and other sectoral requirements would cause severe disruptions in
the economy and lives of the Kenyan people, particularly in the
rural sector. Wood scarcity conditions would undermine rural
stability and development, increasing rural-urban migration
beyond levels which can be sustained by the growth of the modern
sector, which itself would be hurt by wood shortages and oil

import requirements. Beyond the potential shortages themselves lies the prospect for depletion of substantial portions of naturally occurring stocks of woody biomass, with possible negative consequences for the soil ecology of Kenya's most arable lands. This would make efforts to increase food and export crop production, so essential for Kenya's development, exceedingly difficult.

The stock depletion problem has dimensions more serious than indicated perhaps by the 20 per cent cumulative depletion on a national aggregate basis. As shown, the density of woody biomass on cultivated lands would fall by more than 50 per cent by the end of the century. Moreover, as we have discussed, 20 per cent woodstock depletion implies that a much larger fraction of the remaining trees in Kenya will be denuded; that is, left without twigs and branches.

There are, however, as we have stressed, a number of promising areas in which strategic action can be taken. These have been incorporated into the set of targets comprising the Policy Case scenario, introduced and evaluated in Chapter 7. To achieve these or comparable results, programme development must commence as soon as possible, and must be part of an integrated economic, food, and resource planning process. The Policy Case levels of effort can go a long way towards ameliorating the major problems by the end of the century. The gap between wood requirements and supplies can be closed by the year 2000 and oil dependence reduced by 20 per cent. Figures 8.1 and 8.2, below, illustrate these potential achievements. Figure 8.1 shows the pattern by which the Policy Case initiatives could close the wood shortage gap, squeezing it to zero by decreasing end-use requirements through efficiency improvements and increasing the recurrent resource base through various wood enhancement schemes. Without the Policy Case programme, the gap would have been larger in the 1980's and enormously greater throughout the 1990's. Figure 8.2 illustrates this.

The other major achievement of the Policy Case programme would be the reduction of cumulative stock depletion from about 20 per cent in the Base Case to only 4 per cent in the Policy Case. By the end of the century total woody biomass, including the contribution from the proposed wood projects, in Kenya will have been virtually restored to present levels. Moreover, the process of regrowth of naturally occurring stocks will have been well under way as yields from the proposed wood resource schemes substitute in meeting requirements. Finally, the process of restoration and resource enhancement derived from the proposed projects for the 1980's and 1990's, will continue into the beginning of the 21st Century. Thus Kenya will have established a stable and sustainable component of its total energy resource base as it enters the next century.

Realization of a programme of the scope of the Policy Case programme would be an outstanding achievement which would

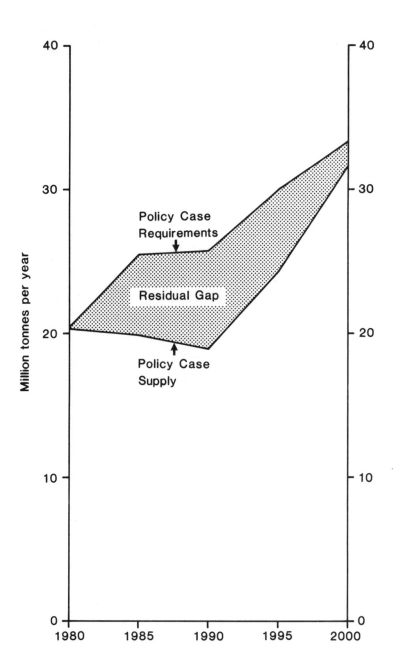

Figure 8.1 Closing the Wood Gap
Wood Supply and Demand

Figure 8.2 Closing the Gap Between Wood Requirements and Supplies

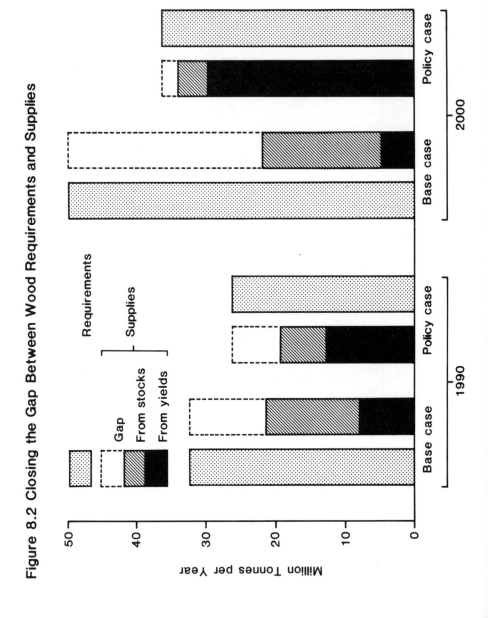

moderate and eventually overcome Kenya's most pressing energy resource and ecological problems. However, even this programme must be considered as a first stage (or baseline) energy plan. Looking again at Figure 8.1 one is struck by the substantial wood supply-demand gap that remains throughout the next two decades until the Policy Case implementations fully close it. The Policy Case targets, though quite ambitious in scope, when measured against the problems facing Kenya over the next two decades are not fully adequate. The difficulties in launching and carrying out such a programme cannot be too strongly emphasized. Clearly, start-up problems will emerge. First, the technical choices and institutional and financial arrangements required for such an effort must be further refined, developed, and put into place. Second, the elements of the Policy Case programme will take time to have their full effects realized. This is especially true for the wood resource enhancement schemes since not all land can be converted at once, and since the stocks of wood need time to mature. These schemes, while contributing somewhat in the near term, have their major impacts towards the end of the century. Thus, even with these efforts, Kenya will be faced with rather serious problems.

The Policy Case Programme (or its equivalent) then, must be understood as a baseline component of a larger policy planning process providing the foundation for that process. First, as the planning and institutional apparatus evolves and begins to refine and implement a baseline programme, it will be necessary to identify and evaluate additional options in order to help reduce near term problems. These might include a mix of the more promising opportunities we have discussed: solar applications (e.g., for drying and other thermal requirements), biogas production from crop and animal wastes (for rural energy uses), producer gas production (for transport, small scale electricity production, and other uses), decentralized power sources (wind, small-scale hydro) and perhaps expanded coal imports. Each of these concepts must be assessed for application to the specific conditions and requirements in Kenya. Each will have its own mix of cost, environmental, and institutional impacts. For example, producer gas implementation could require that additional wood resources be developed as primary feedstocks, and both producer gas and biogas using crop residues could result in loss of soil nutrients. Some of the alternatives may have specific requirements with respect to scale economies and geographic and social contexts. All of them will have costs as well as benefits that must be carefully studied. A baseline set of programme targets such as established by the Policy Case can provide the framework within which this assessment can begin.

In addition to other technology options the opportunity may exist for more rapid near term implementation of some of the elements of the Policy Case programme. For example, as shown earlier, improved charcoal production on a large scale associated

with replanted forests could totally diffuse by 1990.
Implementation of forest replanting itself could be sped-up
during the late 1980's. Furthermore, agroforestry, and forest
management, the other major scheme with relatively early yields,
might be brought on more rapidly. Similarly, at the end-use
stage, improved technologies could in principle be disseminated
more rapidly and/or widely than assumed in the Policy Case
implementation if the institutional, educational, production, and
distribution processes were pursued at a sufficiently high level
of activity.

A final, but critical, dimension of an augmented planning
process is the ongoing re-evaluation of the supply-demand
configuration in Kenya as it evolves. Clearly, the conditions and
dynamics underlying energy requirements and supply render
prediction inherently uncertain. Nor can Kenya's energy future be
expected to unfold smoothly. Moreover, implementation of a Policy
Case programme and its impacts must itself be carefully
monitored, and the evaluation of the results integrated into
reformulations and modifications of the programme as necessary.
The need and opportunities for other options, and the possibility
for expansion and more rapid implementation of the Policy Case
options can be effectively evaluated and implemented only in such
a context. Therefore, the establishment and continuous updating
of a comprehensive resource data base encompassing energy demand,
energy supply, land-use, and food production, must occur if an
effective resource planning process is to become the key element
in national development that the situation requires.

A programme at Policy Case levels, and the larger planning
process elaborated around it, may not guarantee complete success
in resolving the energy and development problems facing Kenya. It
can, however, provide a policy instrument through which the
nation can begin, in part, to take command of its energy destiny,
and with which successes and failures can be measured, lessons
learned, and programmatic reorientations launched.

Wood has long served as the traditional fuel in Kenya.
During the recent phase of Kenya's development the use of wood
and wood derived charcoal as transitional fuels has led to severe
problems which can be expected to grow over time if no policy
action is taken. The failure of wood, and especially charcoal, as
transitional fuels, stems from a number of reasons: the limited
nature of the land and biomass resource bases, rapid population
growth and demographic shifts, the relatively inefficient
technologies employed, the high cost of imported fuel, and the
requirements of development itself.

It has been shown, however, that beyond avoiding crises (of
a social, health, economic, and ecological nature) attendant upon
woodfuel shortages, wood resource management policies at all
stages of the supply-demand nexus could serve to establish a
basis for the transition along the arduous path of modernization
and development that the nation requires. This transitional
process can be assisted by policies aimed at oil import reduction
as well, which have been discussed earlier.

While transition towards a more developed and modern economy could result in a shift towards greater use of more flexible forms of energy such as liquid fuels and electricity, wood resources can be expected to play a large role beyond transition, in a <u>sustainable</u> energy future for Kenyan development. Once such a sustainable resource base and the management and technical skills accompanying it have been established, wood resources and technologies can stand beside more modern fuels like oil, coal and electricity, as well as new and renewable forms such as solar and wind, in a diversified energy system for the nation. Since heavy emphasis on indigenous resources and technologies may be required for some time, various forms of wood derived fuels may find their way into uses in transportation, electricity generation, and industrial production to substitute for or complement the use of other fuels, fuels which are imported or more expensive. Given the continuing uncertainty with respect to oil production, market shares, and prices for the next century, the role of oil itself might remain constrained even as Kenya expands its ability to generate foreign exchange for oil purchases. The enhanced position of wood within Kenya's overall energy supply system, then, could serve two purposes; first to provide a secure baseline fuel as development proceeds, and second to allow a greater portion of scarce foreign exchange resources to be allocated to the variety of non-fuel commodities required for development.

BIBLIOGRAPHY

1. Western, D. and J. Ssenakula "The Present and Future Patterns of Consumption and Production of Wood Energy in Kenya," in Energy and Environment in East Africa: Proceedings of an International Workshop (UNEP, Nairobi, Kenya: 1980), p.365.

2. Earl, D.C., Forest Energy and Economic Development, London: Oxford University Press: 1975. Quoted in Beijer Institute, Proposal: A Fuelwood Systems Model for Kenya, Annex A, p.31.

3. Data for 1978 from World Development Report, 1980, The World Bank, Oxford University Press,1980.

4. Many investigations have shown that it is often substantially less expensive to save a unit of energy; e.g., Roger Sant, The Least Cost Energy Strategy, Mellon Institute, 1979, and Reducing New England's Oil Dependence Through Conservation and Alternative Energy, 1978-2000, Energy Systems Research Group, Report to the U.S. General Accounting Office, 1980.

5. United Nations. Petroleum Exploration in Developing Countries. Graham and Trotman. London. 1982.

6. Development Plan for the Period 1979 to 1983; Republic of Kenya (1979), p.iii.

7. According to the World Development Report, 1980 of the World Bank, in 1977 fuels, machinery, transport equipment and other manufactures comprised 90 per cent of merchandise imports in current dollars. The fuel share rose from 11 per cent in 1960 to 20 per cent in 1977. During this same period balance of payments deficits rose from 34 million dollars to 474 million dollars.

8. Development Plan, loc. cit.

9. World Development Report, 1980, loc. cit.

10. Ibid.

11. Mungale; Machacos survey, described in technical volume.

12. Ibid.

13. K. Openshaw, private communication, 1981.

14. Merz and McLellan, The national Power Development Plan 1978-2000, a report to the East African Power and Light Company, 1978.

15. "Some Facts and Figures on 1980 Operations," EAOR, 1981.

16. Sources: Houre, J.W. and Killick, A., "Future Development Possibilities for Kenya and Their Energy Implications," (in Energy and Development in East Africa, UNEP ERS-3-80, 1980) p. 11 and EAOR, op. cit.

17. Sessional Paper No. 4 of 1981 on National Food Policy, Republic of Kenya, 1981, pp.49-52.

18. Collier, P. and Lal, P. Poverty and Growth in Kenya, World Bank, Washington, D.C., 1980.

19. The detailed process of stock depletion is quite complex, involving demand growth rates, land shifts, regrowth patterns, accessibilities, and so on. This is captured mathematically in the LEAP Model. However, to see the essentially exponential character of the decay process consider the simplified equations:

$$Y_t = a S_t$$

$$\frac{dS_t}{dt} = - (D_t - Y_t)$$

where Y = yields, S = stocks, D = demand, t = years, and a is a proportionality constant (itself a function of stock characteristics and depletion level in the real-world). The equations state that yields are proportional to stocks and changes in stocks result from satisfying demand unmet by yields, respectively. Combining we have

$$\frac{dS_t}{dt} = - (D_t - aS_t)$$

which is an exponential decay form, e.g., $S_t = \frac{1}{a} (D-be^t)$ where b is a constant of integration.

20. See discussion in the Five Year Development Plan.

21. Loc. cit., p. 1.

22. See Technical Volume.

Woodfuel Supply

Supply/ Demand Options	Policies	Adminis- tration	Legislation	Education & Training	R & D	Finance	Marketing & Distribution	Information Publication	Technical Assistance	Self Help	Private Sector	NGO's	External Aid
			Government Strategies									New Government Strategies	
Supply Agro- forestry Farm Woodlots Shelter- belts	Plant trees on farm land to meet rural requirements and assist agric crops Also to establish trees on marginal land & fodder trees on pastoral and rangekinds	Co-operation of Min of Agric, N.R, Energy, Finance, O of President Planning Min of Education	Form Village associations as per South Korea? Pass legislation about free rights on rented land Pass law about planting trees on steep & un- used land, specified by V.A's Establish grants system.	Train extension workers/ officers, teachers. Organise courses for village leaders/ farmers Expand village poly- techs, colleges, universities Include A/F & forestry in school sylabus R & D Cont monitoring tree cover on agric land extension methods	Undertake research in A/F systems tree species shrub species, rotation, thinning, spacing, yield of:- - wood - food/fodder - fertilizer - other prod Mulching trials appropriate tools. Undertake seed trials marginal land viability tests germination methods etc	Set up payments system to give grants to farmers to plant trees. Provide finance for R & D, Education & training publications Obtaining seeds, tools equipment for extension work.	Set up distribution system for seeds & seedling Help farmers market surplus Wood, Food fodder etc.	Produce literature on A/F systems Have radio & T.V.programmes on A.F. Organise schools sylabus Establishing demonstrating centres	Plan A/F programme according to priorities Secure suitable tree species seeds. Establish nurseries & demonstration centres Establish marketing organisations Organise technical material tranis programmes Establish seed orchards	V.A. individual farmers will have to do bulk of planting on own land/ communal	Could Help with seeds, seedlings, marketing of surplus products.	Organise V.A's Do some planting on communal land help with marketing & Dist, Information & Pub, & Tech Assistance	Help with R & D Education & training Tech Assist & Finance Manpower
Replanted Forests	Establish short rotation multi-purpose trees to meet mainly urban and some industrial/ rural requirements of fuel	Co-operation of Min of N.R.Energy, Finance.	Pass laws about formation of parastatal to undertake some of the planting Establish leasing system to enable private companies to do some planting	Train workers, supervisors, managers to undertake planting & extraction Expand all educational facilities	Undertake species trials rotation lengths, spacing, thinning yields, of wood and other products whole tree measurements - shamba, forestry/ fodder work extraction & establishment techniques undertake product market research costing collection & analysis	Secure finance to run entire programme establish system whereby most of income from sale of products is used to run forest service	Establish seed stores, regional & local nurseries, market all products and all parts of trees. Set up yards for wood charcoal and other products	Inform public about planting programmes in each area. Organise school visits for NGO's to plantation areas	Secure suitable tree seeds. Establish nurseries provide people to demonstrate various establishment & extraction techniques. Establish marketing organisation establish seed orchards energy crop	Allow farmers to graze cattle etc. if research shows it is not detrimental	Encourage private sector to undertake some of the planting	Encourage NGO's to do some planting & marketing	Help with R & D Education & training tech assist finance energy crop assistance manpower

Category	Objective	Co-operation	Strengthen	Train	Undertake	This option	Produce literature	Establish marketing	Provide assistance	Allow farmers to graze	Allow private sector	Encourage	Help with
Managing Natural Forests including mangrove & bamboos	To manage N.F. so that they produce more products especially fuel while at same time protecting soil, water, exhance recreational aspect. Preserve as a source of genetic material	Min of N.R.Energy Finance O of P.	Strengthen laws about illegal cutting of & encroachment	Train managers to fully manage N.F. train forest workers in extraction techniques Establish courses in N.F.Man'ment R & D Cont Monitor areas composition & Ecology through KREMU etc.	Undertake thinning, yield, density, regeneration underplanting interplanting grazing water retention & soil conservation Ecology & production of Mangrove, & Bamboos	This option should be self-finance as trees already mature income is used to run service and not going into general fund.	Produce literature about various nat forests open up forests for recreation Demonstrate to public importance of natural forests.	Establish marketing units for all forest products.	Provide assistance for developing management & marketing	Allow farmers to graze if shown to be suitable various	Allow private sector to collect various forests products	Encourage As above	Help with R & D Education Tech Assist & Education Finance Mangrove & Bamboo Management Manpower
Industrial Plantation including farm woodlots for tobacco curing etc.	To encourage industry to use indigenous biomass energy.	Min N.R. Industry, Energy, Land Finance.	Allow land if necessary to be compulsory purchased for energy plantations Establish grant system	Train all levels of workers/ managers.	Research in multi-purpose trees, farm wood lot systems.	Look into possibility of giving planting grant, management grant.	Provide advice publications	Establish seed store & distribution system.	Need private forestry advice monitoring system.		Private sector to undertake planting & marketing.		Help with R & D Education & Tech Ass.
Peri-urban plantations including Road/Railway along towns railway lines trees, Town trees, also trees in towns. To establish energy plantations for irrigation schemes, agricultural settlements	To establish plantations round towns along roads & railway lines & trees in towns. To establish energy crops for irrigation schemes, agric settlements	Min N.R. Energy. Local gov. Land, O of P. NIB.	Compulsory Purchase Establish grant system Form Peri-urban associations of land (PUA) owners to co-ordinate planting & land management	Train all levels of workers, managers in forestry/ recreation/ fodder production & establishing crops on irrigated land.	Research into multi-purpose wood. Animal feed from tree products yields spacing establishing trees on difficult soils, e.g. black cotton soils.	Secure finance to run Gov part of programme & to provide grants to private forestry. Densified wood	Provide publications to others who wish to plant & publications to public who want to explore P.U. forests (recreation)	Establish seed store & distribution system. Help land owners market crops.	Establishment of forest parks. Fodder trees, irrigation roadside planting, urban planting	Plant along roads etc	PUA & private individuals could plant their land.	Assist with roadside, railwayside, town trees.	Help with R & D Education, Tech Ass. Finance Manpower.
Management Of Rangeland Areas	To bring rangeland areas into more production sustained management	Min Agric N.R., Energy O of P	Grant system	Train people to manage these resources, divide areas by priority	Look to ways of managing these areas productively	Secure finance		Help with marketing of products fw, poles gums, fodder.	Rangeland training charcoal production	Co-operate with pastrolists		?	Help R & D & Training

All above programmes will need to be monitored. A costing system from each project should be established, so that payment systems can be realistic. Stumpage rates should also be fixed so as to give an acceptable return on investment, provided costs are kept to a reasonable limit.

WOODFUEL DEMAND

Supply/Demand Options	Policies	Administration	Legislation	Education & Training	R & D	Finance	Marketing & Distribution	Information Publication	Technical Assistance	Self Help	Private Sector	NGO's	External Aid
DEMAND (INTERMEDIATE) EXTRACTION OF WOOD AND OTHER FOREST PRODUCTS	To provide wood and other forest products in convenient sizes and invest possible cost	Ministry of Energy, N.R. Industry		Train sufficient people to undertake R & D and work. ---------- R & D cont. look at whole tree utilization Rosin production Transport costs	Developing hand tools Hand sulkies wood drying research & trials Used of waste-briquetting densifying. Honey product on yields Fodder, food production other crop yield	Provide money for R & D	Look for markets for all forest products. Help with distribution Establish markets co-ops	Produce leaflets about extraction techniques, product collection techniques	Give advice on extraction & Harvesting methods Drying methods tools	Undertake extraction and marketing of forest products	Undertake extraction and marketing of forest products	Assist with extraction and marketing of forest products	Help with R & D Education Manpowers Finance NGO's
WOODFUEL AND FOREST PRODUCTS	To produce woodfuel and forest products of good quality & insufficient quality to satisfy demand	Min of Energy N.R. and Industry	Establish/ Strengthen Utilization Centres	Train people to undertake R & D. Run courses for charcoal production etc. ---------- R & D Cont Density trials on various wood species and on single species at various ages C.Value tests by species, age & moisture content Acetylene production Producer Gas	Chipping wood Densifying of wood. Charcoal production + by products both from pods leaves and wood ash ash. Briquetting of charcoal powder fines Methanol, Chemical, Rosin, Resin, Gums, Boiler Design. Liquid & Gaseous fuel Steam pumps Fertilizer products Fodder product Food production	Provide money for R & D	As Above	Produce leaflets about R & D results	To help with R & D		Could undertake some R & D		Help with R & D Education Manpower Finance

STOVE AND ENERGY CENTRE	M of E Industry	To produce woodfuel stoves with comparable efficiencies to kerosene Gas & Electric stoves. To produce efficient pots & pans		Train people to run centre teach artisans --------- R & D cont Look at uses of wood ash charcoal for cement steel prod. Development of fire lighters Pots & pans. material (clay) Sources Production methods	Fuelwood stoves, charcoal stoves, for H/H & non household use Improve Irons. Look at boiler design for Industry Barn design for tobacco curing, fish smoking, kiln kiln design for pottery/ bricks	Provide money for centre and R & D Provide grants to start small cottage industries	Market surveys, set up marketing systems	As Above Produce literature to explain how establish demonstration centres	To help with R & D Training programmes	Start Cottage industries, small industries	Production of stoves and pots, pans. Introduction of new barns, fish smokers, boilers, etc.	Assist with establishment of cottage industries	Help R & D stove centre Maning and Establishment Education Manpower Finance NGO's
MANAGEMENT	Min Basic Education, Higher education Vocational training. N.R. Agric. Energy Finance	To provide trained people to work in supervise manage advise and do research in the woodfuel supply/ demand options	Establish/ Strengthen teaching & research, training & vocational centres	Train people to man the various educational research centres. Require colleges & university strengthend New Agroforestry forestry centre, utilization centre, stove centre.	All research programmes mentioned above	Provide money for centres and training. Provide money for day release		Produce books, courses, leaflets etc. Pay for house educational programmes	Obtain advice for contents of various course research programmes etc.	Encourage people to attend various vocational artisan courses	Have training levy from industry Encourage apprenti-ships	Use NGO's to organise courses	Help finance colleges, universities etc. Provide manpower for education and research institutes.

Research/Development Strategies To Support Woodfuel Programme

A/F
Agroforestry Systems
Extension Methods
Species Choice
Rotation
Spacing
Thinning
Yields- Wood, Food, Fodder, Fertilizer
Other Products
Mulching Trials
Species For Marginal Lands
Intercropping
Management Of Farm Trees
Monitoring Of Trees On Agric Land
Nursery/Seed Sources - Collection
Seeds - Plus Trees
Viability Tests
Germination Methods
Establishment Methods
Forestry/Species Choice
Multipurpose Trees
Rotation
Spacing
Thinning
Yields - All Products
Intercropping
Inventory & Mapping Methods
Monitoring Of Forest Area
Mensuration Work - Whole Tree Techniques
Economics Of Animal Feed
Bamboo Silviculture & Management
Mangroves
Management Of Short Rotation Plantations
Management Of Natural Forests
Management Of Savanna Woodlands
Establishment Techniques
Work Study/Time Studies
Costing Recording & Analysis
Natural Regeneration Methods
Grazing In Forests
Water & Soil Conservation Experiments
Irrigated Tree Crops
Irrigated Intercropping
Establishment On Difficult Soils
Establishment Under Low Rainfall
Monitoring Of Forest Areas
Monitoring Of Tree Cover On Agric Land
Tool Improvement & Design
Incentive Schemes/Basic Realistic Rates
Felling/Extraction Methods Including Sulkies
Felling/Extraction Costs
Transport Methods
Transport Costs
Whole Tree Utilization
Stampage Price
Needs Three/Four Centres
    To Undertake Above
Agroforestry/Forestry Centre
Utilization Centre
Stove Centre

Utilization
Drying Time For Wood
Chipping Methods
Debarking, Crosscutting Methods
Other Forest Products- Yield And Economics
Rosin, Resin, Gums, Turpentine
Nuts, Honey, Fruit, Food, Fodder
Markets - Price Of Others
Forest Products
Utilization Of Waste
Briquetting Waste, Charcoal
Densifying
Charcoal Production Kilns/Retorts
Methanol Production (Dry Distilation)
Chemical Extraction
Other Liquid Fuels
Gaseous Fuels (Producer Gas
Water Gas)
Steam Pumps
Border Design And Development
Tobacco Barns
Brick Making/Storemaking Kilns
Fish Curing Barns
Fertilizers
Fuelwood Stoves)
Charcoal Stoves) Portable Fixed
Fw/ch Stoves
Pofopan Design
Firelighters
Acetylene Production
Wood Density Determination
Wood Energy Value Determination
By Species/Age/Moisture Content
Charcoal Density Determination
Use Of Agricultural Wastes

Education & Extension
Vocational Courses
Short & Extended Courses
Agroforestry Systems
Establishment Of Nurseries & Trees
Management Of Trees
Tending Of Trees, Felling & Extraction Methods
Tool Care & Maintenance
Management Of Small Industries
Stove Production (Wood, Charcoal)
Charcoal Kiln Techniques
Cottage Industries -Bamboo
Tapping, Collecting Food, Medicine etc
Establishing Demonstration Units
School Farms/Woodlots
Agroforestry - Energy Centres
Woodlots - Energy Centres
Stoves
College & University Courses
Teach Management & Supervision
Agroforestry
Extension
Forestry Plantation
Natural Forest Management
Research Methodology
Teacher Training Courses
School Curiculum
Radio/TV Programmes
NGO Courses. Leaflets